Endorsements

"Barry Ham has great passion for helping couples who have found marriage difficult. For those who are stuck, this book offers practical help on how to get UNSTUCK.

I highly recommend it."

Gary Chapman, Ph.D.
Author of *The Five Love Languages*

"Many couples in America today do not find themselves in deep trouble. Nor, if pressed, do they find themselves at the highest precipice of joy. If they were to sum up their marriage, they might simply use one word—STUCK. Drawing on a lifetime of therapeutic experience and biblical insight, Barry Ham has written an extremely helpful book for couples in any stage of marital development. This book will help you get—UNSTUCK. Read it!"

Graham Baird
Lead Pastor of Mission Street Church, Camarillo, California,
and author of *One Hundred Years of Ministry*

"In this book Barry identifies many of the pitfalls that have contributed to marriages becoming stale and lifeless. But more importantly, he offers clear guidelines and strategies to enable couples to reverse this trend, get unstuck, and experience the marriage that both they and God had in mind."

H.B. LONDON
Pastor to Pastors Emeritus for *Focus on the Family* and author of
Pastors at Greater Risk

"Barry has dialed into the life journey of so many couples, including Christian couples, who really are "stuck" and only "enduring" year after year. The raw honesty and clarity he has captured are both courageous and inviting. But Barry's response to these and other couples has helped them discover that their story isn't over—they get to discover that a new story of healing and restoration awaits them in the grace and truth that Jesus personally invites them into."

BRENT WILLIAMS
Director of Pastoral Care Ministries, Woodmen Valley Chapel, Colorado Springs, Colorado

"Dr. Ham really gets it…long-term, intimate marriage is not based on emotions, but rather on commitment. Our generation has forgotten this fact, and Dr. Ham does an excellent job of providing both insightful and practical suggestions for how to return to this unavoidable truth. Following the roadmap in this book dramatically improves your chance of realizing your dream for a lifelong marriage."

CRAIG CATO
Therapist and author of *Solo on a Tandem Bicycle*

"If you're stuck in a painful and deeply disappointing relationship, there is hope and healing and even possible reconciliation. A well-seasoned counselor and author of *God Understands Divorce*, Barry understands broken relationships and offers practical, compassionate counsel. If you or a friend is "stuck" and sees no way out, this is a must-read. Share it with a friend."

MARK SKALBERG
Creator of the "Starting Over" workshops

"*Unstuck* is real. With stories and examples that most couples will relate to, this book encourages couples to put God at the center and choose to love one another again. For many unhappy couples, the gloom of marriage came out of nowhere, and Barry helps them find the love they always wanted."

Dr. Tim Clinton
President of the American Association of Christian Counselors

"Barry Ham's *Unstuck* is a glorious mess. Barry writes not as a mere theorist but as a seasoned practitioner on the subject. As a marriage and family therapist, he has seen it all. *Unstuck* addresses God's design for marriage and healthy relationships with fresh eyes and an eternal perspective. This book hits the target!"

Jimmy Dodd
President of PastorServe and author of
Survive Or Thrive: 6 Relationships Every Pastor Needs

unSTUCK

unSTUCK

ESCAPING THE RUT *of a* LIFELESS MARRIAGE

BARRY D. HAM, Ph.D

© Copyright 2016—Barry D. Ham

All rights reserved. This book is protected by the copyright laws of the United States of America. This book may not be copied or reprinted for commercial gain or profit. The use of short quotations or occasional page copying for personal or group study is permitted and encouraged. Permission will be granted upon request. Unless otherwise identified, Scripture quotations are taken from THE HOLY BIBLE, NEW INTERNATIONAL VERSION®, NIV®, Copyright © 1973, 1978, 1984, 2011 by Biblica, Inc.™ Used by permission. All rights reserved worldwide. Scripture quotations marked NASB are taken from the NEW AMERICAN STANDARD BIBLE®, Copyright © 1960, 1962, 1963, 1968, 1971, 1972, 1973, 1975, 1977, 1995 by The Lockman Foundation. Used by permission. Scripture quotations marked NLT are taken from the Holy Bible, New Living Translation, Copyright © 1996, 2004, 2007 by Tyndale House Foundation. Used by permission of Tyndale House Publishers, Inc., Carol Stream, Illinois 60188. All rights reserved. Scripture quotations marked GW are taken from the GOD's WORD Translation, Copyright © 1995 by God's Word to the Nations. Used by permission of Baker Publishing Group. All emphasis within Scripture quotations is the author's own. Please note that Destiny Image's publishing style capitalizes certain pronouns in Scripture that refer to the Father, Son, and Holy Spirit, and may differ from some publishers' styles. Take note that the name satan and related names are not capitalized. We choose not to acknowledge him, even to the point of violating grammatical rules.

DESTINY IMAGE® PUBLISHERS, INC.

P.O. Box 310, Shippensburg, PA 17257-0310

"Promoting Inspired Lives."

This book and all other Destiny Image and Destiny Image Fiction books are available at Christian bookstores and distributors worldwide.

Cover design by: Prodigy Pixel

For more information on foreign distributors, call 717-532-3040.

Reach us on the Internet: www.destinyimage.com.

ISBN 10: 0-7684-0853-9
ISBN 13 TP: 978-0-7684-0853-9
ISBN 13 EBook: 978-0-7684-0854-6

For Worldwide Distribution, Printed in the U.S.A.

1 2 3 4 5 6 / 20 19 18 17 16

Contents

	Introduction	11
Chapter One	The Ideal Plan	15
Chapter Two	How Did We Get Here?	31
Chapter Three	Going Under the Radar	49
Chapter Four	Throw in the Towel or Endure	65
Chapter Five	Commitment—A Different Approach	81
Chapter Six	Lessons from Success—Engagement	99
Chapter Seven	The Critical Puzzle Piece	117
Chapter Eight	Wild Blue Yonder	133
Chapter Nine	Relearning the Dance	153
Chapter Ten	Where Your Treasure Is	177
Chapter Eleven	Seasons of Change—Preparing for the Storm	195
Chapter Twelve	Remembering	209
	Appendix	221
	Notes	223
	Acknowledgments	231

"Just because the past didn't turn out like you wanted it to, doesn't mean your future can't be better than you've ever imagined."

—Unknown[1]

Introduction

"While the threat of divorce may appear to be the major motivation for change, the threat that the relationship will remain the same is far more powerful."[2]

Why are you reading this? You may have picked the book up off the shelf because the title or the cover caught your eye. Perhaps you were online searching, stumbled across this, and ordered it. Or it may have been recommended or loaned to you by a friend. Those are all good pieces to the answer, but the question remains—why are you reading this?

While I most likely have not met you, I can make some educated guesses. In all my years as a marriage and family therapist, I have yet to have someone call me and say, "My marriage is in terrific shape and my spouse and I are thoroughly enjoying life and each other. We just had some free time on our hands so we thought we would see if we could make an appointment to come in and just chat. We saw your picture on the Internet and thought you looked like you would be a nice person to meet."

People come to my office because they are struggling with relationship issues. Things are not going as they had anticipated and now their marriage may be in crisis. They need help and they are looking for answers. My guess is that you are reading this book because you feel that your marriage is far from what you had dreamed it would be. You may have envisioned a spouse who would fully accept you, emotionally support you, treat you with grace and kindness, and, well, love you like no other. Yet the point in time arrived, whether it was a year ago or this morning, when you realized: "This is as good as it is ever going to get." You may have contemplated divorce but are petrified by the prospect of how your children will be impacted, ways that your family might react, or how you would survive financially. Perhaps you have been married for decades when you came to this "status quo" realization and it seems too late now to get out. The bottom line seems to be—you're stuck!

My guess: this is why you are reading this book. You feel depleted, dejected, perhaps even rejected, and you don't know what to do. You are tired of settling for what feels like a loveless relationship. You want to experience the fulfilling marriage of which you once dreamed. What you have now does not ignite your spirit or feed your soul. You want more!

The quote at the beginning captures the motivation that can be generated by the threat of divorce. Still even in a divorce, good or bad, there will probably be some kind of change. But this—this empty stuckness is miserable! Being alone is one thing, but being alone in the context of a marriage, having to face the constant reminder of your disconnectedness, can be all-consuming.

You are reading this book because you no longer want to be stuck. You desire a life that is vibrant and energized. And I am here to tell you, it can be. You don't have to settle into relational rottenness. Neither do you have to escape on the next ship to some isolated island on the other side of the planet. Life can be different—very different. Your marriage can be reignited and rejuvenated. Will it be?

Introduction

That I don't know. But what I do know is that many couples have been able to adopt successfully the principles set forth in these pages, and they are now doing life very differently—and loving it.

So, if you are tired of being stuck, I encourage you to travel through these pages with me. The potential gain is immeasurable.

"Many people spend more time planning their wedding than they do planning their marriage."

—Zig Ziglar[1]

Chapter One

The Ideal Plan

Wow! Could this really be happening—finally? Doug and Annie were standing among the aspen trees, with the sun shining brightly, as they were about to recite those treasured words: "I do." It was a picture-perfect day in Colorado, with their family and best friends all part of this anticipated occasion.

This had been a long time coming, as they had been dating for a few years. From the time of their initial meeting, their relationship had experienced a variety of twists and turns. Doug had been working for a large nonprofit business in a public relations position. He had enjoyed this work immensely—perhaps even more so when Annie joined the company, becoming his supervisor. They quickly hit it off as friends and found their ability to collaborate in business to be both personally satisfying and beneficial to the organization.

Neither of them was looking for a romantic relationship. Annie had recently ended a disappointing long-term relationship and was more than content to be doing life "unattached." While Doug had not been in a relationship for a few years, he also had found solace and even a peace in focusing on his work and hanging out with his friends and his dogs (not always necessarily in that order).

However, as is often heard said, "when they least expected it," things took a sudden turn—for the better. Annie was transferred to another branch of the company. While she had always enjoyed Doug's company and thought he was attractive, she never really considered having anything but a friendship with him. She had strong principles when it came to appropriate workplace relationships, especially since she was his supervisor. However…now that she was no longer in that role…hmm.

That summer, during the company-wide barbeque, the two of them had the chance to chat, catching up on both work and personal developments. And it was during this conversation that something happened. While they weren't quite sure what it was, they both left the evening with a new perspective on possibilities. The following weekend, they went out to dinner for the first time—well, the first time as an official date. A spark had ignited, and they were both, as they called it, "smitten."

Over the next few years, their relationship grew to a level of health and connectedness neither had believed possible, and they were thrilled. They were frequently heard to comment to their friends, as well as each to other, about just how "easy" this relationship seemed to be. Following the past challenges of other relationships, this seemed like a dream come true.

So, here they were, four years later, preparing to say their wedding vows to one another. Annie looked gorgeous in her dress, and Doug cleaned up pretty well too. Their families liked their respective son- or daughter-in-law-to-be. The dream they both had nearly given up on was about to become reality. This was perfect!

For most of us, we find ourselves reading this story and thinking, "Yes! This is what it is supposed to be." We have read and reread stories of the knight in shining armor who rescues the beautiful damsel in distress. From the time that we were children, we have heard tales ranging from "Sleeping Beauty" to *The Princess Bride*—and they all seem to end with "happily ever after." That is what we want—the fairy-tale love story with the happy ending. Over time this vision has become ingrained in our brains. This is what we want!

However, the experiences of most of us have been far from these rosy narratives. Even so, deep down inside, if we are honest, we still long for the kind of love and relationship that is described above. Why? Where does it come from? Is it a cruel hoax that has been woven into our psyche? Is it remotely achievable? If so, how in the world do we find it?

The Design

As we journey together through these pages, we will endeavor to answer these questions—and many more. But let me begin by assuring you that yes, these desires have been implanted deep inside our souls, and no, this is not some cruel hoax.

Individuals have reasons for wanting to get married that run the gamut. While we usually imagine that "love" is the great motivator, that is not necessarily always the case.

Not surprisingly, "expectations" is frequently cited as the impetus behind marriage. It may be that a person's family expects their son or daughter to be married by a certain age because for generations, family members may have fulfilled that unspoken role. This, in turn, can make that person feel as though if he or she is not married by that magical age, then something must be wrong with him or her.

About twenty years ago, I was in Japan visiting my friend Mike and his wife, who had traveled there to teach English. An interesting term I discovered was when they referred to a woman as a "Christmas cake." I was puzzled by this until he explained to me the tradition. The idea is that if one has cake on Christmas, while it is sweet and tasty, nobody really wants it after December 25th. If a young woman isn't married as she approaches thirty, she is viewed as "left on the shelf too long" or "past her expiration date." In other words, she is in danger of becoming a "Christmas cake."

I recall years ago in California working with a young woman who had heard the message loud and clear, "If you are to attain your rightful place in this family, then you will get married and give us grandchildren." Expectations, oftentimes communicated using guilt, can be a strong motivator.

Along the same lines as family expectations may be self-expectations—beliefs that "I am about to be too old and will no longer be 'marketable'." I hear this especially from women who feel that their best days are behind them and all that lies ahead are wrinkles and sagging body parts: "Before long, no man will find me attractive and I will be destined to wander through life rejected and alone."

Another incentive for marriage might be "someone wants me." While there is nothing wrong with being wanted (that is a good thing), it is the fear of not being wanted and perhaps even winding up alone that leads some people to jump at the first opportunity. Consideration may not be given as to whether or not this is a good match because the prospective bride or groom is worried that he or she won't find a match at all. They reason that someone (whomever it may be) is better than no one.

Being "complete" is often a subtle and unspoken incentive for marriage. There is a misguided notion that "if I am not married, then I am not complete." For these individuals, marriage is seen as the highest status of existence. How many times have you encountered someone who has never been married and viewed him or her with pity? Our unspoken logic is "that poor thing. Her life just can't be full and complete unless she has a mate." Continuing that logic: "And if she can't be full and complete, then she must be unhappy and is probably even miserable. Oh, what a shame. I feel so sorry for her. I certainly don't want to be viewed as pathetic so…I guess I had better get married."

The Ideal Plan

There are any number of reasons that compel us to marry, some wise and others not so much. But it is no accident that my deepest longings include a desire for a spouse, a partner, a helper, a person who knows me better than anyone else and loves me anyway. We come by this desire quite naturally.

Marriage, contrary to the opinion of some, is not an invention of man. It originates from the Creator of man. The One who designed us, who knows us best, placed within our makeup, within the fabric of our DNA, a longing for "another."

Look at the Genesis account of creation, where we see God acknowledging the fact it was not good for man to exist alone (see Gen. 2:18). Marriage is God's idea. He brings together a man and a woman to unite them in the first marriage.

In Genesis 1 we have the account of God's authorship of you and me and creation. You get a summary statement at the end of the first chapter in verse 31: *"God saw all that He had made, and it was very good. [So] there was evening, and...morning—the sixth day"* (Genesis 1:31). Everything He had done He said was good. But you read a little bit later and the phrase "not good" enters the picture. Chapter 2, verse 18: *"The Lord God said, 'It is not good for the man to be alone...'"* (Genesis 2:18). Now, what's the context of that? You flip back to the first chapter, to verse 26, and you read, *"...Let Us make man in Our image, in Our likeness, and let them rule over the fish of the sea and the birds of the air, over the livestock, over all the earth, and over all the creatures that move along the ground"* (Genesis 1:26).

We've got a scenario here where God has created out of nothing, calling matter into being. He is creating, not out of a sense of need or out of a sense of boredom, but out of the reality of His character. Now in the midst of all that, you've got Scripture stating that everything is good; yet there is one thing that's not good—that the man should be alone (see Gen. 2:18). You see, God is about relationship. We go back to Him saying "let Us," meaning "Us" within the Godhead. As Father, Son, and Holy Spirit, there is a perfectly sufficient community; there is complete relationship. God created men and women, not out of a need for a relationship, but out of a desire. He yearns to relate to human beings, and He has placed within us that same innate desire to relate—to Him as well as to each other.

So you've got God creating a finite human being to bear the image of an infinite God. For that to happen, plurality has to enter the picture. There's no way that one man, one woman, one boy, or one girl can bear His likeness. Yes, we all carry the thumbprint of God individually, but our ability to reflect God's image happens most fully when plurality enters the picture. Plural—not just one individual, not just male but female.

As a result, regardless of your personality type—you can be the biggest introvert in the world or the biggest extrovert; it doesn't matter—we all have the same flashing indicator light for intimacy on the dashboard of our hearts. It is a yearning for fulfillment that God has placed in our awareness. We have this innate understanding that we need each other.

Out of this context comes "the design." Within various cultures, marriage traditions may look very different from one another. One country may have arranged marriages while another, like the United States, champions the right and ability to select one's own mate. Even within this country, we may find wedding traditions that entail simple church ceremonies, couples meeting with the justice of the peace, or elaborate, multiday feasts and events. Practices of how marriages come together vary, but the intrinsic desire to be bonded, connected, wedded happily and permanently comes directly from the heart and makeup of God. It is not by accident. "...*God created* [man] *in His own image...*" (Genesis 1:27).

The Ideal Plan

All I Want Are Two Things

I was shocked a few years ago as I listened to a group of single women in their forties and fifties discuss their criteria for dating candidates. I will readily admit that I was a bit naïve, but I was stunned nonetheless. I expected to hear that they would marry for love, compatibility, and so on. Instead, they listed items such as "six-figure incomes" and "someone who could fund all their travel desires."

What do you most desire in your marriage? Is it the two-story brick house, the fully funded pension, or the vacation condo? Or is it something more relational?

In my years as a marriage and family therapist, I have found—and my own personal experiences would support this—that people generally want two things. Just two? Yep. Now you may be guessing, but I want to encourage you, before you read further, to search deep within yourself for what these two things might be. I mean, at your core, the things that would fill you the most, the longings you have had since you were a child—what would they be?

For most individuals, when they feel safe enough to take the risk and put it out there, they say this: "I want to be fully known and fully loved." You may be looking at those words and wondering why I am emphasizing them so. You may say, "Well, sure, that makes sense. I would want that." But think for a minute about what I am saying.

"I want to be fully known." As a kid, I felt like no one understood me. My parents thought that…well, that I was a kid, that what I thought was silly, that my desires were immature and my feelings were to be dismissed. My siblings weren't much better. And my friends—oh, my friends. I wanted that "best friend"—the kind that Scripture refers to as *"closer than a brother,"* the kind that *"loves at all times"* (Proverbs 18:24; 17:17). Yet those who would be my friends might hang out with me one day and appear to be loyal, only to belittle and make fun of me and talk viciously about me the next day. They probably thought that I was weird and went to find other friends.

"I want to be fully known AND fully loved." There is the rub. While I want to be fully known, to do so I run the risk of being ostracized and abandoned. So, I let you know me—sort of, but not fully. I protect myself and avoid being vulnerable. I allow you to see the good parts of my personality, the parts that you might like. If I show you only the attractive, generous, magnanimous me, you may stick around. However, even if you do stay close, I will know that you are doing so because you think that you know who I am. Truly though, you know only a part of me. When you "love" the picture of me that I have painted without really knowing all of me, the love feels empty.

If I am honest, I want to be BOTH fully known AND fully loved. I have longed for a lifetime to have someone know me—good stuff, flaws, blemishes, warts, idiosyncrasies, weirdness and all—AND when she does, to completely, unconditionally love me! Think about it—isn't that really what you desire? Wouldn't that be the ultimate relationship?

We typically either let someone know us completely, which can be a very frightening experience, or we paint an unrealistic picture of ourselves that we think perhaps someone will love. Either way it feels hollow.

Now I recognize that only God is capable of knowing and loving without conditions, and we will look more at that in a later chapter. But I would contend that most of us have grown up longing for that kind of relationship with another human being.

I remember reading the book *The Shack* a few years ago. If you read it, you may have loved it or hated it for a myriad of reasons. There were certainly components of it that rattled against the traditional bubble edges of my Christianity. But the thing at which I thrilled was the relationships between Papa (God), Jesus, and Sarayu (the Holy Spirit). Getting a glimpse of what the relationship within the Godhead might be like was exhilarating! Why? Because I long to relate to others like that. I long to be known for all that I am—the good, the bad, and the ugly—and then to be loved with a love that doesn't stop, to be admired like there is no tomorrow, to have a loyal partner and companion for all of life.

Isn't that the image that fairytales paint for us? Isn't that why we repeat those stories over and over again? As we began to be aware of the opposite sex, aside from just the hormonal drives, weren't we looking for that individual who would finally love us with a knowing love, a love that we had always desired but never obtained? As we talk about and ponder the "ideal," isn't that it?

Rarely does anyone approach marriage hoping for less than the "ideal." I have yet to meet anyone who says, "Well, it's time. I guess I am supposed to find a mate. I don't care much what he is like. Actually, it would really be great if, after five or ten years, he would talk down to me, ignore my desires, and trample on my feelings. You know, the more I think about it, that would be perfect. That is really what I am looking for!"

If someone said this, we would think that he or she had a screw lose. If we knew that was what we had to look forward to, we would quickly run in the other direction. Nobody desires that. We desire a connected, satisfying, absolutely rocking relationship. Yet I see more and more marriages that are anything but that. They are dissatisfying and unfulfilling. I don't know about you, but I don't want that. I suspect that you don't either.

The Vows

My guess is that if you're reading this book, you are doing so because your marriage is less than ideal. It is not anything like the marriage that Doug and Annie began with at the beginning of this chapter —YET. But there is hope! Yes, you believe in the "ideal" about which we talked about—or at least you used to. You recognize the fact that there is an inner longing at the root of your being to be connected to that person, to have a love that is unbreakable. And the discussion of wanting to be fully known and fully loved resonates with every fiber of your being—if you are honest enough to be vulnerable.

You ache for this kind of God-designed relationship. This desire is nearly always reflected with some pretty serious wedding vows.

Over the years, I have been privileged to conduct numerous wedding ceremonies. Walking alongside a couple oftentimes begins with premarital counseling. It can be an incredibly energizing journey for them as they make this wedding come to life. Watching as two people pour out their love for each other in the birth of a new life—*"the two* [shall] *become one"*—is exhilarating (Matthew 19:5; Mark 10:8; 1 Corinthians 6:16; Ephesians 5:31).

I work closely with couples to custom-design their ceremony. While some pastors have a pretty tried-and-true service that they like to use, I prefer to give couples the opportunity to make it richer and more meaningful by putting a flavor of them into it. After all, it is their wedding.

I have officiated weddings that have looked extremely different from one another. Some couples want to include a poem that was a favorite of their grandmother. Others wish to incorporate special phrases or thoughts they have heard in another ceremony. Still others have a particular Scripture or reading they want included.

Wedding ceremonies may utilize a unity candle or sand ceremony, participation by parents or grandparents, or even children or pets. I have seen a wide variety of components. The wedding vows may be traditional or more contemporary. You get the picture—there can be lots of variety.

And yet, even with the unlimited possibilities of looks, most ceremonies still exhibit some basic similarities around words of commitment.

I like to include two sets of vows. The first one is a commitment that is made before God and witnesses (family and friends). For example: "I ask you, Doug, do you have this woman to be your wedded wife, to live together after God's ordinance in the holy state of matrimony; do you promise to love, comfort, honor, and keep her in sickness and in health, and forsaking all others, keeping only unto her as long as you both shall live?"

Everyone who is present is a witness to the commitment that was made. God is also in attendance as well. We are making some serious, covenantal statements. These are actually statements for which we can, in some sense, be held legally and morally accountable.

The second set of vows, while still made in front of God and others, is really a more specific group of vows that one individual makes to the other. These vows are substantial, and they are personal. While the first set of vows is typically responded to with "I do," the second set of words is spoken by the bride and groom to each other. For example: "I, Annie, take you, Doug, to be my wedded husband, to have and to hold from this day forth, for better, for worse; for richer, for poorer; in sickness and in health; to love, to cherish, till death do us part, according to God's holy ordinance, and thereto I pledge you my faith."

While you may have heard these phrases repeated dozens of times, contained in the singular sentence above are words of enormous depth and significance. Again, we utter them because we want the "ideal" in marriage, and I sincerely believe that most people want to mean them. Let's look for a moment at just what it is we are committing to.

We are promising with the force and reputation and enduring truthfulness of our word. In that sentence we have promised to take (have) this individual as our spouse and to hold him or her with a secure and lasting love in three sets of circumstances: for better, for worse; for richer, for poorer; and in sickness and in health.

I find it interesting that we don't typically say, "for better *or* for worse," as often the words used are "for better, for worse." Now you may be thinking, "What is he talking about? 'For,' 'or'—what's the difference?"

Think back to when you stood in the front of the church, the gazebo in the backyard, or the overlook at the Grand Canyon. You were gazing at your spouse-to-be, heart beating quickly, thinking, "Wow! He is the most handsome man on the planet" or, "She is radiant and stunning." As you recited these vows to each other, you probably thought about the three circumstances described above more in the following terms: "To have and to hold from this day forth, for better, for worse"—*oh my goodness, she is the best. This could never be worse. I am so fortunate to be marrying her. Of course I will commit to this circumstance. It is easy because it will always be better*—"for richer, for poorer"—*he has a great job and is a hard worker. I know some people that get married are poor, but we won't have that issue. We are doing fine financially, and this will always be good*—"in sickness and in health"—*I am standing here looking at this beauty. She seems to be in pretty good health to me so I know this won't be an issue.*

In other words, we find ourselves basically making a commitment more like this: "Of course I will embrace him forever. I will love him for better, for richer, and in health. I can do that." And, as long as that boat isn't rocked, we just might be able to do so.

Unfortunately, we need to go back to that word *for*. Why do we use that word? Because we are not committing to "better or worse," "good or bad," "easy or challenging"; we are vowing to do both. You see, while today at our wedding it may be better, you can be assured that somewhere along the way it will be worse. Making a commitment to when it is good is not that difficult. Promising to love when it is extremely difficult—"for worse"—now there is the real commitment.

Promising to be there for your spouse when he or she is rich—does anyone find that a tough promise to make? It is like having a discussion with the bank about paying your credit card statement on time after you have just won millions in the lottery—not too much of a challenge. But how about having that same conversation with them following a major layoff, when you are out of work with no job prospects? In your vows you are acknowledging that along the way, there will certainly (at least for most couples) be some hard, maybe even devastating, financial hurdles ("for poorer"). There is a meaningful promise.

And what about our health? "Well, if he is healthy, I can certainly promise to continue to embrace him." That is easy. Let's make it a little more realistic: "I promise to be there, loving him even when he is sick with the flu." Or "I will unwaveringly cherish her even when she is experiencing her monthly cycle." That's a start. How about when he has a disabling blood pressure condition or she has a complicated pregnancy? Or when she has Alzheimer's or he has Parkinson's disease?

You see, as we stand at the altar, drinking in the vision that stands before us, the last thing that we are pondering is "worse, poor, and sick." And yet, that is where the rubber truly meets the road. That is where genuine lasting commitment takes place. There will be worse. There will be poorer (financial obstacles and challenges). And if we live long enough (although it may not even require advanced years), there will be sickness—I promise.

The Hope

Like most people, you came to the marriage altar with some hopes. While you may not have fully understood God's plan or His design, you knew that marriage was one of the core components of family and community. You came to it planning for a lifetime with your mate. It is for this reason that we make promises before God and to each other to be loving and faithful for a lifetime. Whether we had seen parents who were happily married or who stayed together but were miserable, we knew that WE wanted something that was loving, lasting, and fulfilling!

Most of us carried with us hearts that longed to be FINALLY completely accepted. We were ready to have the "someone" whom we had chosen to fully know everything about us and to have that person unconditionally wrap their arms around us, holding us close with a tender, understanding, and treasuring love. Oh to be fully known and fully loved!

With those hopes and desires in place, we made promises of lifelong friendship and faithful companionship through the most challenging of circumstances, which most of us will encounter in our marital journey.

But then something happened—a change occurred: the wheels slowly began to come off the bus, and we found ourselves possibly having feelings of guilt, second thoughts, or regrets. We may have tried to ignore the problems and pretend that all was well. But our guts told us—maybe screamed at us—otherwise.

I see this with couples in my office on a weekly basis. They have avoided acknowledging what is caving in around them until there is little left to hang on to. Then they call in crisis, desperate for help. Perhaps you are tackling issues before you get to that desperate place.

Regardless of where you may be in the journey, I want to assure you that there is hope. God has indeed wired you for companionship. His design for partnership will work. Our longings are innate and with purpose. And we can make promises that are possible to follow through with—and I don't mean in a grit-your-teeth-and-gut-it-out manner. I am talking about promises that, even when difficult to keep, can be rich, fulfilling, and, as strange as it may sound, pretty exhilarating.

If you are depleted by your journey, I encourage you to read the chapters that follow. My goal is help you turn your seemingly energy-draining "death march" into a life-infusing adventure.

"Placing blame in marriage is like saying,

'Your side of the boat is sinking.'"

—Hank Smith[1]

Chapter Two

How Did We Get Here?

"This is perfect" is exactly how Doug and Annie began their marriage, and it indeed seemed like a dream come true. Their first few months together could not have been more blissful. Doug was thoughtful in the small things—opening the car door for her, bringing her the occasional bouquet of flowers, and texting her often during the day. Annie, too, was attentive to Doug's needs—leaving sweet love notes in his lunch, sitting next to him as he watched his beloved college games on television, and, his favorite, giving him backrubs after a day of yard work.

But then, ever so slightly, like the subtle course change of a cruise ship, things became, well, different. An entire work day went by without any communication from Doug. Not a big deal. Annie knew that most of her co-workers didn't hear from their spouses during the day so she figured that she had just been spoiled and guessed that this was normal. But she still felt a tinge of disappointment.

As football season cranked up, Doug was really looking forward to his alma mater's first game of the year. However, as he was getting ready to watch it, he learned that Annie had made plans with her girlfriend for that afternoon. Not a big deal. Most men that he knew watched the games by themselves or with a buddy. While he missed her not being there, he also figured that it must be normal.

"Not a big deal." And these situations weren't a big deal. But what seemed to be minor issues grew with time. Eventually, all the attentiveness to small details began to evaporate. It wasn't long before the new "normal" became Doug doing "his thing" with his friends while Annie was absorbed with her hobbies and interests.

It was not as though things were bad between them. They still enjoyed each other's company. It was just that their times together were less frequent. Occasionally, they found themselves missing the way that it used to be, but they were each reassured by their respective friends that this was normal. As a matter of fact, some even intimated to them that their closeness as a couple and their awareness and sensitivity to each other's needs weren't normal. So, they accepted the drift that was forming between them. But if they were honest, they didn't like it. The problem was that they weren't honest with themselves—and certainly not with each other.

Silently, without awareness of what the other was feeling, relationally undermining resentments began to form. In the early days of their marriage, they would have talked about these feelings, but not now. Complacency had set in, and neither one knew what to do. But again, verbalizing their feelings had become a casualty of what too many of their friends called "normal."

At home in the evening, they were still cordial, but it no longer felt like the intimate connection for which they had both married. They were each beginning to feel a loneliness that ached almost more than being alone. When they had been single, being alone was to be expected. And alone was not always lonely. But now they were married—not exactly alone, but feeling lonelier than ever.

Sitting with her friend Sheri at Starbucks one day, Annie broke into tears as she poured out her pain, as well as her disbelief, to her friend. "How had this happened?" she wondered aloud. She felt foolish, thinking that she had somehow missed the warning signs, that she should have seen this coming before she married Doug. She had longed for the "ideal plan" about which she had read in Scripture. What had happened?

While fishing with his best friend Cliff, Doug grumbled about how quickly his relationship with Annie had grown stale. Certainly Doug realized that things would change. I mean, he had seen the passionless relationship of his parents. He just thought it would be decades from now before that happened. As he talked about his frustration out loud, he realized how angry he felt. He had been so very careful and intentional in his premarital conversations with Annie. She knew the kind of relationship for which he had hoped, and yet, now he was abandoned—or so he thought.

As Doug and Annie explored their disillusionment with their respective friends, they found themselves asking the same question again and again: "How did we get here?"

Doug and Annie aren't alone. Far too many individuals married with the "ideal" in mind, only to find themselves sitting in this very place.

This Isn't Supposed to Be

Sitting in my office on a fall afternoon, I listened as my client Frank grabbed a tissue and stated—actually, pleaded: "It wasn't supposed to be this way!" He was talking about the condition of his relationship with his wife and his grown daughters. Following another evening of verbal abuse from him, his wife had walked out. While this wasn't the first time they had separated over their years of marriage, something about it felt more…final.

He talked about his life and what was "supposed to happen." He had always thought that his marriage would be more connected, that his children would love and respect him, that his boss would appreciate his skills and efforts at work. Yet the picture he was painting was anything but that. As a result, he was stuck. He couldn't see any hope. He couldn't envision any possibilities. He was in a deep, dark place, unable to see any way out.

As I listened, it became clear that while all of these relationships were important, it was the one the he had (or didn't have) with his wife that was truly his undoing. His disconnection with her was taking the wind out of all his sails. Over and over he would proclaim, "This isn't supposed to be!" And he was right.

If we accept God's design for marriage from the previous chapter, and all the inviting possibilities that go with it, then Frank is absolutely right—"this isn't supposed to be!" And yet, at one time or another, we have probably felt exactly as he did.

I wonder, what are your "supposed to be's"? By that I mean, what have you envisioned in life that you assumed was an absolute—that was just naturally going to happen? Perhaps when you were growing up you believed that your parents were always supposed to be generous and understanding. After all, they were parents, and you expected them to behave in a certain manner. Yet many of us have experienced a household that was very different.

Maybe you always thought that after you were done with your formal education, some employer would naturally hire you, appreciate your talents, and pay you well. Has that happened consistently—or ever?

But certainly, when it comes to a lifelong mate, you had visions of that one person with whom you could be naked and unashamed, that person who would fully know you and, in spite of your faults, would fully love you. Let's face it—I think that before we were married, we all thought it was "supposed to be" that way.

But just as Doug and Annie learned, we may wake up one day and wonder, "What the heck happened?" The reality of our marriage is often a far cry from the dream that we pursued.

One might think that it is only in modern history that we have arrived at this disillusioned, cynical place regarding marriage. But I would suggest instead that it is a disappointment that has a great history to it.

In the nineteenth chapter of the Book of Matthew, an encounter is recorded between Jesus and the religious leaders of the day. They are asking questions about marriage and divorce from a bias that implies that marriage is not necessarily permanent. However, in His response, Jesus is quite clear that from the beginning, marriage was always designed to be a committed, lifelong relationship. He basically says that from the dawn of creation, God's plan was one man, one woman—together for life (see Matt. 19:1-6).

His disciples seem a bit surprised by this when they say in verse 10, *"If this is the situation between a husband and wife, it is better not to marry"* (Matthew 19:10). Even today some suggest that since people are living longer, it is somehow unreasonable to think that a person can be faithful to the same person for forty, fifty, or even sixty years. Tim Keller states that "belief in the desirability and goodness of marriage was once universal, but that is no longer true."[2] Yet I would submit that the values reflected in Scripture around the subject of marriage are really the deep longings that we have always had.

I appreciate Scott Stanley's words: "Sometimes people fault God for seeming to impose a harsh or unreasonable ideal on us, yet what we really want deep inside is the very thing that He designed. The problem is not with the vision; it's with the fact that it's hard to attain."[3]

Perhaps in that statement is the challenge. The vision is good and embodies all that we desire. However, we often enter marriage without the skills, tools, and understandings needed to attain it.

Therefore, it is hard—perhaps brutally hard—to attain. And with that realization, we are gravely disillusioned.

She's Not What I Thought

Chandler had met his wife while stationed in South Korea. The first few years of their marriage seemed to progress without too much disruption. Relationship roles that were modeled for her in her family of origin were typical for her culture: the woman's role was more subdued and passive, and the husband was the authority in the home. So, she made her needs subservient to his. This arrangement worked for Chandler as he liked being in charge and having a more dominant role in the family. As he stated, "She let me pretty much do whatever I wanted. I thought this was great. We had what I felt was really a pretty good arrangement."

Following the end of his deployment, he and his wife moved back to the United States. As one can imagine, it didn't take long before Chandler's wife was exposed to very different role expectations. Whether it was through the wives of his friends or American television, she began to learn that marriage in this country was not about, as she put it, "superior and inferior."

Up to now, he had been able to run his household by edict and even intimidation. Oblivious to his wife's crushed spirit, he operated thinking that things were working just fine. All the while his wife's resentments festered, alienating her from him and placing unseen strain on their marriage. It wasn't until their teenage son ran away from home that she was finally able to verbalize, for the first time, her distaste for her husband. She even had thoughts of moving out. He was shocked.

As he sat on the couch, he relayed his stunned disbelief that his marriage had gotten to this point, proclaiming, "She's not who I thought she was." While this may seem an extreme case, arriving at this declaration is not.

Humans having been making this statement in one form or another from the beginning of time. In the biblical account in Genesis, the paint is hardly dry on the creation canvas when we begin to see this mindset rear its head. The serpent has just finished tempting Eve to eat of the Tree of Knowledge of Good and Evil. She convinces Adam to share the fruit with her when their dream world begins to come apart. They instantly realize their sin and set out to hide from God (as if that were possible). When finally confronted by their Creator with their disobedient choice to eat from the forbidden tree, Adam throws Eve under the bus. He tells the Lord, *"The woman You put here with me—she gave me some fruit from the tree, and I ate it"* (Genesis 3:12).

Can you imagine that conversation? Adam implies, "You know, things were going okay, Lord. I was naming the animals, You and I were chatting at night in the Garden, and everything seemed to work. Then You put this woman here. Well, I guess after a while I got used to the idea. You told me that this was for my benefit, that I needed a partner. Yeah, I guess I did like having her here, and she was pretty amazing to look at. I figured that this just might work and be a positive arrangement. But then look what happened. Look at this sin thing. I mean, I thought I could trust her, but it is obvious that she is just not who I thought she was."

Once we proclaim that "she is not who I thought she was," a host of possibilities are introduced: "If she is different than I expected, then maybe I need to rethink this marriage thing. If she is not what I was counting on, then the logical implication is that I should probably look elsewhere until I find the one who will be. It would seem that the answer to my disillusionment is to rethink (and rewrite) my vows and perhaps to retract from my commitment."

It is for this very reason that our country has seen such an upswing in couples living together rather than getting married. The feeling often is that if I don't fully commit myself in marriage, then I am somehow able to avoid risking as much. In an effort to avoid pain and disillusionment, I hold back. However, the results of this approach are that I wind up risking even more.

Research studies repeatedly demonstrate that cohabiting couples experience less security and greater anxiety. Many men have figured out that they do not need to recite marriage vows in order to receive some level of companionship, sex, and reduced living expenses. With this arrangement now in place, women often begin to feel that they have little to gain in marriage and have the "illusion" that there is a lot to lose. As Mike McManus states in *Living Together: Myths, Risk & Answers*, "Women cohabit to get a marriage proposal. Men cohabit for sex and money."[4] Of course one of the consequences of this thinking has been the increase of unwed Americans. From 1970 to 2003, that number has grown from 21 million to 52 million.

Since there is no definite sense of commitment in cohabiting relationships, there is a greater likelihood of unfaithfulness than there is for a married couple. Another study of 309 couples found that even when cohabiters do get married, they report a lower degree of marital satisfaction than those who have not lived together prior to marriage.[5]

While disappointment in who I have discovered my spouse to be is certainly discouraging, failing to make the marriage commitment would only have served to increase my anxiety and insecurities.

He's Not What I Thought

As my wife sometimes tells me, "You just can't make this stuff up."

I met Jack and Nicole as they arrived for their initial appointment on a snowy February evening. They came in trying to laugh and make light of their need for counseling, while a tension hung in the air.

They had met at a poker table in Vegas and were married twenty-eight days later. Now before you think, "The foolishness of youth!" I need to tell you that they were both in their early forties.

The issue that had driven them to counseling was new discoveries. Nicole knew that Jack had a child from a previous relationship. However, it was when she recently surprised him at work to take him out to lunch that there were new revelations. She found him talking with a woman who was also a previous girlfriend with whom he had fathered another child. Her world came crashing down.

Although it may be easy to sit on the outside and pick out the red flags—meeting at a poker table, only dating twenty-eight days before getting married, having undisclosed children from previous relationships, and so on—they had managed to miss them.

Nicole sincerely believed that she had found the man of her dreams—outgoing, charming, and fun. While complete trust in him may have been ill-advised so quickly, she did trust him—that is, until the revelation. But now, from her place of devastation, she found herself shaking her head and telling me, "He's not what I thought."

While I recognize that this may seem an over-the-top example, the statement she made is much more common than one might think.

When Brad and Julie first began to date, life was one big party. They readily admit that their dating relationship was a whirlwind, which included "too much alcohol, too much sex, and too little communication about things that mattered."

Now they were eight years into their marriage with a four-year-old daughter, feeling as though they had no common ground on which to stand. While they were certainly experiencing a plate full of differences, the one that was unraveling them might not be what you would expect—sex. You see, even though this had been a major focus of their relationship early on, Julie thought it would change after marriage. It wasn't that she didn't want intimacy with Brad;

it's that she *wanted* intimacy with Brad. In other words, as is often the case, she had engaged early on in a sexual relationship in order to get love and closeness. Brad had engaged in sex in order to get, well, sex.

Now that she wanted a deeper, more connected relationship, she was surprised to learn that he wasn't all that interested in greater intimacy. She thought that after marriage, he would just naturally want to grow in this manner as well. This was part of her vision for marriage, a piece of her picture of what her husband, her ideal, would be. Here she sat, dejected, feeling hopeless, declaring, "He's not what I thought. I expected something—someone—different. He is not the man I had hoped he would be."

Nicole and Julie, like so many women, found themselves lamenting, "How did we get here? This is not how it was supposed to be. I expected a spouse who would long to know me and pursue me with love. Instead, I am lost, afloat on an ocean of disappointment, and thoroughly disillusioned—maybe even disgusted."

I'm Not What I Thought

Who are you? This is probably a question we have been asking ourselves since we first became aware of "self." So, what do you think—who are you? As young people, we often tried to define ourselves by any number of things—the clothes we wore, the sports we played, our hairstyle, or the crowd with which we hung out. So, who are you?

Leaving home and going off to college may be the first tangible evidence that indicated a true element of independence, that made us feel as though we could actually make it on our own. Did we "find ourselves" in college? We made friends, again becoming part of a crowd. We picked majors, and we continued to try to either confirm our image of self or reshape it. How did we do? Some began to form an identity, while others remained lost.

I have known individuals who seemingly wander their entire lives without really having a solid sense of self. Often these people will marry—perhaps marrying someone else who is equally unsure of his or her identity. Then together, they muddle along. When this happens, the two "selves" are often defined more by their reactions to one another than they are by themselves. As a result, people will make statements such as, "She brings out the worst in me" or, "I didn't used to be this way until he came into my life." But I wonder how accurate those claims really are.

I own a 1985 Firebird, having bought it in July 1985. It has been a fun car with lots of memories. However, after over twenty years and nearly 250,000 miles, it was time to park it and get something that made a little more sense to drive in Colorado. The Firebird was tired, the engine no longer pulsed with the power it once had, and the transmission was slipping. I would drive it once in a while, but about five or six years ago, it mostly just sat in the garage. I knew that I would save my nickels and dimes and eventually begin to put it back into shape.

A couple of years ago, I began to do that—by having a rebuilt engine and transmission put in it. Once again it came to life and was drivable. Yet it just didn't seem to have the get-up-and-go that it should have had, and it didn't run very smoothly. I drove it for less than 500 miles when the engine blew. Not what I expected after waiting all this time. But the shop pulled out the engine and put in another one. Now it runs smoothly and with power, as it should. But what happened to the old engine that it only lasted a few hundred miles? The engine manufacturer discovered that there was a crack in cylinder number four.

There is a process involved in rebuilding an engine called "magnaflux," a procedure where technicians use liquid and pressure to find any cracks, no matter how small. But somehow they had missed this one. As a result, as the car was driven, the crack only got bigger and more exposed until the engine would no longer perform.

Similarly, I see couples in my office who seem to be doing fairly well in their relationship until pressures come—the kids are in trouble; there are financial concerns or in-law issues. The list of possibilities can be lengthy. However, here they sit, with their thoughts as to what they think the problem is (which is rarely the real issue). Just like with the engine, there are underlying cracks in the relationship that existed all the time but were not visible until the pressures came. The pressures simply exposed the cracks, the problems that were there all along—the miscommunications, the lack of attention to the relationship, the self-centeredness, the unkindness, and so on.

In the magnafluxing process, the pressure is supposed to reveal the cracks so that the appropriate steps can be taken to avoid the very problem I experienced. Pressures in our marriages and relationships can serve the same purpose: they can be an opportunity to reveal areas of weakness so that we know where to focus our efforts and attention in order to improve our relationships.

While we may want to think of ourselves as kind, generous, loving, patient, and a whole host of other virtues, especially toward our spouse, I wonder if that is an accurate picture. Like impurities rising to the top of a refiner's fire, the natural magnafluxing processes of marriage will give us the most accurate picture of who we really are. It may confirm that we possess these qualities or it may reveal cracks that are larger than we ever imagined.

When that happens, we may, shaking our head, groan, "I'm not what I thought." And with that realization comes disappointment, disillusionment, discouragement, and perhaps even a sense of hopelessness and despair.

Grieving the Loss of the Dream

How utterly depressing! "I got married with optimism overflowing. Finally, I believed, it would be smooth sailing. But my reality bears no resemblance to the dream, which has completely unraveled.

There were visions of what was "supposed to be," but those idyllic images have been dashed against the rocks of reality. Rather than a life of love and fulfillment, I have experienced the fact that I am living with a stranger. He or she is not at all what I believed him or her to be. But perhaps even scarier is the fact that I am a stranger to myself. I believed that I would be a good mate—and I seemed to be, as long as everything went smoothly. But once life began to settle in, I was shocked to discover who I actually am. No wonder we have difficulties—I wouldn't want to be married to me." How do we respond?

With a cynical view of marriage, many opt out. An interesting label that I have heard recently from senior citizens is the term "paramours." This label refers to individuals who are in what I would call a "relationship of convenience." They become a "couple," oftentimes choosing to live together but not to marry. These relationships provide some level of companionship—but without any of the constraints of marriage. The couple may benefit from the sharing of expenses for a period of time, but there is an understanding that should either one get sick or develop more significant needs, they will separate—the individual's children or someone else will have to be responsible for their care.

"Paramour" seems like such a sweet name for a relationship between two eighty-year-olds. But I would contend that it is not what any of us really desire. If my heartfelt longing is to be fully known and fully loved, it will require an "all-in" investment by someone who will be there through the "worse, poorer, and sicker." I want someone who will be by my side through all of life—from the riding of Pirates of the Caribbean at Disneyland to the holding of my hand as I take my final breaths.

And yet—you may have recently awakened from your marital slumber to discover that the dream has been shattered. Now what? Do you give up? Do you try to start over with a new relationship? This book is not about throwing in the towel just yet. It is a book that

I hope will stretch your imagination as to possibilities—possibilities for your own growth as well as for change and hope in your marriage. We will begin to explore ways to do this in the coming chapters. My promise to you is this: if you hang with me through these pages, I will show you ways to do your life and marriage differently.

Necessary Steps

In the summer of 2014, Colorado Springs experienced the "Black Forest Fire." It was the most destructive fire in Colorado's history. Hundreds of homes were lost and lives were uprooted overnight. I had friends who lost their homes and everything that they owned.

Out of those ashes, homes are beginning to rise again. Of course, it hasn't been easy. The sifting through the ruble, the obtaining of various permits, the clearing of once beautiful but now dead pine trees—the contracting and rebuilding—is a long and arduous process.

Yes, some have given up and moved on. But for those who have decided that rebuilding is worth the diligent effort, beautifully restored homes are appearing—in some cases, homes that are more beautiful than those that were originally built. But before that could happen, there were steps that individuals and families had to negotiate. They first had to grieve the loss of their dream. Whether losing a home to a fire or losing a marriage to disillusionment, the grieving process is similar.

Step 1—Address your utter shock and disbelief. Following the fire, families were stunned that the homes in which they were watching television twenty-four hours earlier had been reduced to a pile of smoldering embers. This may be a familiar feeling to you as you read this wondering how the relationship you dreamed of has become another relational casualty.

I sat with a client this week as he reeled from being served divorce papers by his wife. While the marriage had been in serious trouble for a couple of years, he continued to try to rationalize that it wasn't all that bad. Obviously it was.

Acknowledge the reality of where your relationship is. It may have sprung a few leaks or it may be submerged like the Titanic. Wherever it is on the spectrum, call it what it is. Honestly assess its condition.

Step 2—Realize that anger and sadness are okay. I hear individuals sometimes say that they "shouldn't be angry," that anger is a negative thing. However, anger is a real emotion and is sometimes very justified. Even the Bible recognizes that emotions are just feelings that are not to be denied, but embraced (Eph. 4:26; John 11:35). The emotions themselves are not a problem, but what we do with them could be. As you ponder your unfulfilled hopes and faded dreams, you may experience overwhelming anger. I urge you to carefully avoid unleashing your anger at your spouse. This will not serve you well. Instead, I encourage you to find a trusted friend or therapist to help you gain some perspective on these feelings.

At the same time, sadness may also be very appropriate. Let's face it—if your ship has sunk, if your house has burned to the ground, or if the proverbial wheels have come off your marriage, it is sad. It is VERY sad. And you will likely find yourself depressed. That is logical given your situation. If you weren't sad, I would be more concerned. And yet, this sadness is not a place to camp. Untended it can become like quicksand, sucking you deeper and deeper into the abyss. However, an authentic sadness that drives you to reevaluation and change can be of great and lasting benefit.

Step 3—Accept where you are. By this I certainly don't mean that you should be satisfied with the miserable place in which you find yourself. What I mean is, accept the reality of your situation. If my client who was served the divorce papers this week had been willing to accept the reality of his situation sooner, it may have moved him to action before his marriage deteriorated to that point.

Honesty is a great place to be. You may not be sure how you got here. You may be disillusioned because what you are living is so far away from what you had dreamed. You may have discovered that both you and your spouse are not who you had envisioned. But there it is. Take a step back. Observe it, analyze it if you choose, ponder it, grieve it—but recognize and take a picture of exactly what your situation is. By all means, it doesn't have to remain there. But for now, fully grasp and own what it is. It may very well be a pile of ashes right now, but possibilities await.

"A bizarre sensation pervades a relationship of pretense. No truth seems true. A simple morning's greeting and response appear loaded with innuendo and fraught with implications. Each nicety becomes more sterile and each withdrawal more permanent."
—Maya Angelou[1]

Chapter Three

Going Under the Radar

It was a typical Saturday afternoon at home. Doug was cleaning a few things in the garage while Annie ran some errands that had been piling up all week. Doug was lost in his thought world as he reflected on his conversation with Cliff and began contemplating what his role in their marital disintegration might be. Yes, Annie wasn't responding to him as he had hoped. Their life together was certainly not the fantasy partnership that he had envisioned. But Cliff had challenged him by suggesting that Doug may not be the "knight in shining armor" that Annie was expecting either.

Those words stung at first. He had been convinced that he was doing all the things that would be expected of the ideal husband. But as Cliff continued to prod, Doug began to catch a glimpse of possible tarnish on his imaginary armor. Here he was, alone with those thoughts.

At first he was angry, feeling that somehow Annie had made him this way or had created this scenario. But the more introspective he became, the more he realized his less-than-stellar role as a husband. He needed to broach this subject with Annie. The spiraling disappointment had gone on for long enough. He would speak with her tonight.

Following dinner that evening, Doug asked Annie if they could talk for a minute. With a slight roll of the eyes, expecting another lecture about some perceived failure on her part, she consented. Doug knew that she was less than anxious, but he pressed forward.

"Annie," he began, "I know that next month we will be celebrating our first anniversary." She stood silent as he continued: "I also recognize that this first year has been…well…not exactly what we had planned."

"You can say that again," she replied. Her sharp response increased his tension and blood pressure.

He continued: "I was just thinking that perhaps we could talk about how we have both dropped the ball during this year."

"Oh, so I've dropped the ball now?" she snapped.

"Well…I just meant…"

"No, I know what you 'just meant'," she said. "You just meant that I am a failure, that I am not the perfect wife—you've only told me a hundred times—that I am not what you pictured, that I'm not…," and on she went with her litany of flaws.

Doug did his best to contain his building frustration. "No, I wasn't saying that only you have dropped the ball…"

Again she jumped in with resentment that had been percolating for months: "Oh, but you are saying I have dropped the ball. I know what you expected—a sex goddess, a gourmet cook, and a cleaning lady who would never question anything you did."

With that comment, Doug started to leave the room, turning back to face her as he was in the doorway. "You are impossible! This is why we are where we are. There is no reasoning with you. You say the most ridiculous things and are completely irrational. I was a fool to even try to talk with you. I don't know what I was thinking, but I sure won't make that mistake again."

With that he slammed the front door as he headed toward the car and the beginning of his stealth journey, his efforts to be invisible. Still inside the house, Annie broke into tears and reached for the phone to call her mom, repeating to herself, "I don't know why I even try to talk with him. But it won't happen again. No, I will never allow myself to be vulnerable to him and his harsh criticism ever again!"

Enemy Attack

"Flying under the radar" is a term that originated in the military in the 1950s. In order to avoid the enemy's radio detection system, planes would fly at a lower altitude, where they were more difficult to detect. With today's enhanced electronic detection systems, the military has developed planes like the Stealth Bomber to counteract those measures.

We frequently talk about "flying under the radar" in our relationships, using the phrase to indicate our desire to stay out of trouble—whether that be a teenager in relation to his parents, an employee in relation to her boss, or a husband in relation to his wife. We avoid being detected by our perceived enemy in order to sidestep problems. While this is an important military strategy, it is quite sad when it becomes a marital one. We no doubt have to wonder how in the world our spouse—this person with whom we longed to spend every waking moment for life—became our enemy from whom we strive to protect ourselves.

I am often amazed at the stories I hear about the lengths that some individuals will go to in order to "stay out of trouble." One client recently recounted how she had decided to participate in an activity that she knew her husband was against. They had discussed it numerous times, with the conversation sometimes becoming quite heated. She had boldly stated that it was something she was going to do, whether he liked it or not. But then when she actually made the decision, she kept it from him—for seven months.

One day while he was downtown, he saw his wife from a distance. In a conversation that evening, he casually mentioned that he had seen her downtown. Knowing that he would be upset with her, she lied and said that he must be mistaken, that she hadn't been down there that day. Like a fighter jet under enemy attack, her brain was racing to figure out how not to get shot down. She was trying to dive to a lower elevation to get under the radar. Actually, she had been endeavoring to stay under his radar for seven months.

However, she was found out. Through a chain of events that evening, he learned that she had lied to him. And, as is often the case, the lie was worse than the original deception. The broken trust that they brought into a counseling session drove their therapy in an entirely different direction of intensity.

A few years ago, I had a couple taking my "Marriage and Family" class at the university together. In the course of a discussion about honesty in communication, she reported that a few years earlier, he came home one night with a boat. A what? Yep, you heard correctly—a boat. He had been checking them out for some time. He had been looking at boat magazines, talking to boat owners, visiting the marina, and so on. It wasn't like she didn't know he had an interest in boats and would someday enjoy owning one, because she did. But in discussions, they both knew that it would not fit into their financial picture for several more years.

Yet he wanted what he wanted—a boat. He knew that he couldn't tell her what he was thinking and planning because they had agreed that this wasn't the time for that purchase. So, he would go look on his own, getting financing information on the sly and making plans without telling her. He was trying to stay under the radar and not create trouble for himself. Of course, you are probably thinking (and correctly so), "How can you bring a boat home and remain undetected?" Well, that is where the plan broke down—and so did the trust in their relationship for months to come.

In both of the stories above, it was interesting how the guilty parties tried to defend their positions. The husband who discovered his wife going behind his back felt that she had been lying to him for seven months, while she only believed she had lied about being seen downtown. The husband who bought the boat said that he had only violated the agreement when he actually brought the boat home. However, his wife felt that he had been less than honest about his intentions and had been deceiving her for months.

The bottom line is that when you are on the receiving end of "under-the-radar" strategies, you feel deceived, discounted, disrespected, and most importantly, betrayed. And that can be an emotional deal-breaker.

Sometimes avoiding detection is about deceiving our mate in a way that allows him or her to believe that something is that isn't. I had a couple a few years ago who had planned for their retirement years to be spent living abroad. During their twenty-five-year marriage, the husband would frequently talk with anticipation about what it would be like when the kids were grown and they were retired and free to travel and live in various cultures. During the past couple of decades, she had decided that this wasn't really an attractive option anymore. However, each time he would eagerly bring up the topic, she would just smile and nod. She had no plans of their ever living abroad, but she continually allowed him to believe that they were on the same page because she didn't want to risk an explosion by having an honest discussion. But of course, doing this didn't prevent any coming eruption; it only delayed it. And the conflict-avoidant behavior only created a deception that made the eventual revelation even worse.

Other times, staying under the radar is about feeling that one is not good enough in the relationship. I recently read an account of a husband who always felt inferior in his marriage. His wife had a knack for putting him down and expressing what a failure he was at every turn. He would do his best to please her, only to be told how, once again, he hadn't made the grade.

One year as Christmas approached, he searched long and hard to find her the perfect present. He so wanted to please her and get her approval. He eventually found a beautiful red dress that he could envision her wearing, and the picture in his mind was one of stunning beauty.

On Christmas morning, he waited with anticipation as she opened her present. It was immediately clear from the look on her face that he had once again failed. Her words were even worse, as she harshly expressed what a "boneheaded choice" that was. She said that any husband would know that his wife wouldn't want a dress like that. He was crushed, but rather than have an honest discussion, he apologized and chose to take an under-the-radar approach.

Of course, in doing so, he buried his emotions, which grew into resentment. Those resentments in turn festered until any feelings of desire for the relationship were gone. It was not a huge surprise when this marriage eventually unraveled for good.

Perhaps I Can Wait It Out

Many couples on the brink of unraveling come into my office with icicles in the air. Tamara and Ken were no exception. While they had been married for over fifteen years, the last five had taken an isolating turn. Sexual conflict had been an ongoing issue for the two of them. Challenges pertaining to frequency, time of day, and lack of intimacy outside of the bedroom had all been struggles for them.

One particular evening, Ken had approached Tamara, wanting to initiate sex. However, feeling distant as a result of an argument earlier that morning, Tamara rebuffed his overtures. For Ken, this was one rejection too many, and something inside him went cold. He decided then and there that he would not approach her for sex again—she would have to come to him; she would have to make the first move.

For the next couple of weeks, Tamara didn't notice much out of the ordinary, except that Ken seemed a bit less talkative. She just chalked it up to their busy schedules. However, as two weeks became two months, she became irritated at his uncommunicative state. As this continued, something inside her began to die as well. She made the conscious choice that until he began to talk with her, he could forget sex. And there they sat.

Ken was intent on waiting her out. He honestly believed that by withholding communication, he could make her crack and she would somehow be forced to initiate sex. Of course, it should come as no surprise that this ploy did not seem attractive or inviting to her. At the same time, knowing his strong sex drive, she thought that she could break him first. Until he began to communicate, she would do nothing to encourage intimacy.

They had become like two children sitting across the room from one another in their respective corners with their arms crossed, determined to outwait the other. They really believed that by doing this, they could break the resolve of their mate. They remained in their determined positions for five years. Then they came to see me.

Feeling unloved, rejected, unattractive, and disrespected had taken its toll. Trust was broken and dreams were vacated. They had determined to not risk any more, to stay under the radar, to wait for the other to make the first move of love and desire. But the move never came. As a result of their attempt to not risk self, they came to my office dragging a lifeless marital corpse behind them. By not risking any more, they had actually risked everything—and lost. Waiting it out had not panned out.

I am reminded of the well-known story of Jonah trying to wait things out. In the biblical account, we read that God had given Jonah instructions to go to the city of Nineveh to preach against the wickedness of the people (see Jon. 1:1-2). However, Jonah did not want to go. He was not a fan of the Ninevites, perhaps in part because of their wickedness. He was actually okay with the fact that God was going to destroy them. But rather than tell the God of the universe that he wouldn't go, he decided to fly under the radar.

The text reads in Jonah 1:3: *"But Jonah ran away…"* He tried to skip town—went down to Joppa and caught a ship to Tarshish (see Jon. 1:3). He honestly thought that it would be that simple to fly under God's radar. Perhaps God would forget about him or lose sight of him. Maybe God would let go of this whole notion and Jonah would be off the hook.

Thinking, "There is no pleasing my husband or wife," I wonder how many times we have headed to the basement, the bar, or the gym to wait things out. "Maybe he will forget about the conversation we had yesterday." "If I can hide out long enough, she might not remember how angry she is at me." Yet this rarely works.

In Jonah's case, things took a nasty turn. He found himself in the sea, swallowed by a giant fish (see Jon. 1:17). It is interesting how quickly he went from hiding from God to engaging in meaningful conversation with Him. Having your life flash before you can have that effect.

It is not unusual for your attempts at hiding to result in your being found out as well. And, as we have seen earlier in this chapter, being discovered trying to hide from your spouse is often more destructive than staying honest and at least attempting to engage. While many would say that they work to remain undetected because their spouse will never change, I have seen on more than one occasion individuals laying low for the opposite reason—because they fear their spouse will change.

This was exactly the fear experienced by Jonah, and it became a reality. He went to Nineveh, proclaimed God's word, and the city repented. *"When God saw what they did and how they turned from their evil ways, He* [had compassion] *and did not bring* [upon] *them the destruction He had threatened"* (Jonah 3:10). Now you may be thinking, "Wait, isn't that a good thing?" Of course it is, but just because Jonah obeyed God and confronted the people didn't mean that Jonah wanted them to repent. He still wanted them to be destroyed. I think he enjoyed preaching against them and blaming them for all that they were doing wrong. When God spared the city, Jonah was angry. You see, if God showed them grace, it just might mean that Jonah's attitude toward the people might need to change, and he was not at all interested in that.

I see couples who, on a regular basis, come in thinking that I wear a black and white striped referee shirt. They want to point blame at each other and have me decide who is the greater offender. Of course they claim that they want the other person, who is obviously in the wrong (in their mind), to realize they are in the wrong and change. Yet if that in fact happens, the proclaimed victim is often left speechless. The wind has been taken out of the individual's sails. Each liked his or her anger. Each felt justified. "How dare you change as I have asked! Now I can't be mad at you. And, of course, if I don't have a reason to stay angry with you, then I might have to relate to you. I might have to reengage with you and risk some of my emotional self. That feels dangerous, and I don't want to do it."

It is easy to understand that, whether in war or in marriage, "flying under the radar" is about safety. We may have felt severely wounded by our spouse and, as a result, we are afraid to risk any more. We are looking for emotional safety. But what if the enemy wants to call a truce? What if our mate waves the white flag? What if he or she is repentant and apologetic and works to make needed and genuine change? Then what? "Hmm… I would probably have to come to the table and open up myself and own my stuff as well." And yes, that can be intimidating. "So," we ask, "can't I just stay under the radar?"

Flying Low

Flying low and remaining undetected is sometimes our best strategy for staying out of trouble. We are doing our best to not be destroyed by our perceived enemy. Again, while this may work well in war when flying behind enemy lines, operating in this manner in a marriage rarely leads to success. As a matter of fact, over time it will often lead to the destruction of our relationship and perhaps even our own moral integrity.

Over forty years ago, while in college, I married at the anything but ripe age of nineteen. Although many had tried to warn us that we were too young and that teen marriages had a low rate of success, we were convinced that we knew better than those who were older and further down the road of life. We had seen the struggles in the lives of our own parents but were convinced that we would avoid all their mistakes. I think we bought into the fantasy that we would lovingly gaze into each other's eyes, never have disagreements, always want and be interested in the same things, and, well, have the perfect marriage that no one else had been able to achieve. And we nearly pulled it off—but then day two started.

Like Doug and Annie and many of you reading this, we quickly learned that marriage wasn't as easy as we had anticipated. We discovered that those eyes into which we had gazed were not always attractive, and we got tired of looking into them. We did have disagreements (tons of them), and our interests often felt as though they weren't just dissimilar, but polar opposites.

I remember the month and the year, following a particular argument, when I made one of those bold internal statements, thinking, "I'm done trying to connect with this unreasonable woman. I have had it. That is the last time I make that attempt." While it wasn't really the last time I made attempts, it was the beginning of a decline into getting below the radar. And that nosedive became not just about trying to stay out of hot water; it became a pattern of dishonesty and deception.

It began with the omission of information—not giving the complete story, withholding important details. It grew to bending the truth so that I could get and do what I wanted without being questioned or having to be accountable. As I got by with deception, it emboldened me to continue to "manipulate the truth" (a nice-sounding phrase for lying). My selfishness grew, and I began to rationalize and justify my behavior: "It is really her fault that I have to live like this. If she were not so unreasonable, bossy, critical, demanding, _____ (you fill in the blank), I wouldn't have to lie to her." This is the kind of logic I sometimes hear when talking to victims of domestic abuse: "If you didn't do (some behavior), I wouldn't have to hit you."

It is a sick and twisted logic. If someone describes it to us as I have above, it is pretty easy to spot the absurdity of it. However, when we get there in inches over time instead of at a pace of one hundred yards per day, we are not so quick to identify the spiral into irrationality. I learned to do the inches journey well.

Convinced that I was the victim, that I was mistreated, that I was unloved, that I had been kicked to the curb, the next step in the progression was all too easy. I needed to connect with someone "who understood me," someone who cared, someone who would fulfill that fantasy I described earlier. And I did.

Just as the lying became easier over time, so did the cheating. It was fun, and I felt alive (at least for a few moments at a time). The Apostle Paul talks about this mindset in the first chapter of the Book of Romans. He describes the progression to a desensitized, depraved mind (see Rom. 1:18-32). We would probably never make that journey knowingly. By that, I mean if someone said to you, "Will you intentionally lie to your spouse?" or, "Will you betray your spouse by having an affair?" we might answer, "Absolutely not!" But when it is a rationalized step-by-step journey down an ungodly path, anything is possible.

I had fooled myself into believing my own press. I had convinced myself that what I was doing was…perhaps not exactly okay, but certainly justified. I was deluded, and it all began with a "fly-under-the-radar" mentality. My honest moments with myself were becoming more and more scarce. But on those rare occasions when I did have them, I knew that in the interest of remaining undetected, I had evolved into a hollow existence. I had definitely wandered from the relational places where God wanted me to be. I had lost my decency and integrity. I had lost myself.

I wish I could say that I woke up before too much damage was done, but that was not the case. It took going through a divorce nearly thirty years ago and watching the lifelong damage that was being done to my children before the hardened shell around my heart began to melt.

I am so very grateful that God broke through my defenses with His grace and redeemed that "wretched man" part of me. But oh, how I wish I could have spared others the pain caused by my self-centeredness. How I wish I had learned to choose a path of engagement over one of deception.

Stealth Attempts

As you read this chapter, I encourage you to ask yourself, "How am I diving under the enemy's tracking system?"

A few years ago I sat with a major college basketball coach and his wife, who were mired in their stealth lifestyles with one another. Their journey into disconnection had been in place for some time. As a college sports figure, he received the adulation of donors and fans alike. At the same time, his wife, who was a respected figure in the medical profession, continually received praise and gratitude from hospital staff and community outreach organizations. They reminded me of a scene from the movie *Fireproof* where Kirk Cameron's character is baffled at how he can receive such respect from co-workers in the fire department, as well as from his friends, but so little (or no) respect at home from his wife.

This couple was in that place. And the greater the accolades they received on the outside, the deeper their stealth dive was on the inside—in their marriage. They both had begun to find connection and some level of fulfillment outside of their relationship with each other, and their continued deception was taking them down a path that neither had intended. Because of their attempts to "stay out of trouble," they were about to watch their world implode. While they were capable of preventing it, to do so would require that they risk vulnerability, something that neither was willing to do.

So, I ask the question again: How are you avoiding detection? Has your world become one attempt after another at being Teflon-like, trying to get nothing to stick to you? Do you do your best to fill up your time with people, things, or activities so that you don't have to risk exposure with your spouse?

I have seen individuals fill their lives with hours upon hours of gym workouts, race cars, golf, model railroading, kids' sports, a daughter's beauty pageants and acting endeavors, weekend alcohol binges, volunteering, drug use, television, cigar smoking, pool, hanging out with their same-sex friends who "understand" them, and yes—even church activities. Now don't get me wrong, I am certainly not saying that all these activities are detrimental. What I am saying, though, is that if any of these are designed simply to escape and hide from my spouse, to keep me from engaging, then they are dangerous.

Just such a danger occurred on March 8, 2014, when much of the international news coverage became focused on Malaysia

Airlines Flight 370. It was a flight from Kuala Lumpur, Malaysia, that was bound for Beijing, China. The flight consisted of twelve Malaysian crew members and 227 passengers. Contact with the airline was lost less than an hour after takeoff.

Following the airplane's disappearance, searches of mammoth proportions were conducted without success. News organizations speculated with numerous theories as to what might have taken place and where the plane may have crashed.

One report noted that the plane had at one point ascended to 45,000 feet (about 10,000 feet above where it should have been flying) and then quickly descended to about 5,000 feet. It explained that this maneuver might have been executed for the purpose of avoiding radar detection. Unfortunately, while that move may have accomplished its purpose, it also may have doomed the flight.[2]

Similarly, many of us have taken extreme measures to protect our emotional selves, to avoid being discounted and criticized by our spouse, to stay out of trouble. We may have tried to make a calculated move taking us from 45,000 to 5,000 feet, only to find ourselves in a dive so steep that we are unable to regain control before it is too late. Flying under the radar is a ploy that seems logical when we are reeling from the wounds inflicted by our partner. However, its success is usually limited in time and scope. The risks may be greater than anticipated.

We met the person of our dreams and embraced him or her in marriage. We looked forward to spending our lives with this idealized figure. But then we learned something about our spouse and ourselves: all was not as we had hoped. Disillusion swept over us like a devastating lava flow. Knocked back on our heels, we retreated. We learned to pull back. We learned to minimize risks with our mate and began to fill our lives with other distractions that we hoped would bring us happiness and keep us from being a target. And yet, if you are reading this, I imagine that approach has met with limited success. So, what do we do now? How do we get by? How can we endure?

"A relationship is like a house. When a lightbulb burns out you do not go and buy a new house. You fix the lightbulb."

—Unknown[1]

Chapter Four

Throw In the Towel or Endure

Their first anniversary came and went with little fanfare. Oh, they marked the occasion by going out to dinner and pretending that it was a celebration of their marriage. But inside each of them, something had died. The bright hope they had shared seemed a distant memory. Doug and Annie muddled through year two, but they both had managed to resign themselves to the idea that this was as good as it was going to get. Their dreams of intimacy and partnership had deteriorated into a semi-peaceful coexistence.

Now, I don't want you to think it was awful all the time. The couple still had fun moments, but they were fewer than either one had thought possible when their love first began. Annie had dreamed of fireworks; Doug hardly even lit a match. Doug had envisioned a Technicolor journey; Annie seemed to do life in black and white.

By their fifth year of marriage, two children—a two-year-old boy and an eight-month-old little girl—were keeping them occupied. With the arrival of each child there were glimmers of hope that this new human life might somehow spark new emotional life into their relationship. However, as the novelty of the changed family dynamics wore off, they slumped back into their ho-hum life together—but now with the added stress of a newborn.

As the children grew, Doug and Annie's life became filled with shuttling kids to and from soccer games, piano recitals, gymnastics, back-to-school nights, birthday parties, and other activities and events. If you have had children, you can probably relate. Life was busy. Life was filled full, but it was not fulfilling. The two of them had poured themselves into their kid's lives. While Doug would take their son fishing, Annie would indulge their daughter in a day of shopping. They each wanted their children to have the best—to have life better than they did as children.

But what was most interesting to watch, and what was probably subconscious on their part, was how the two of them approached their kids' relationships. As both of their children began to date, Doug and Annie seemed to take a special interest in coaching them. They would warn them of red flags and point out characteristics in their children's dating partners that they saw as troublesome. It became clear to the outside observer that Doug and Annie were doing their best to make sure that their children did not wind up with what they had—a disappointing, passionless existence. They longed for their kids to have the perfect hope-filled partnership that they had been unable to achieve.

Once both kids went away to college, Doug and Annie were left with each other. Over the past twenty years, they had done life in a self-absorbed, disconnected manner. While that seemed to provide some level of emotional protection, they were now even greater strangers to one another than they had been when the kids were born. In their efforts to "not feel" so that they wouldn't be hurt by the other, they both had unknowingly contributed to what was now a frightening loneliness.

Petrified by the prospects of the future, they found themselves retreating further and further into their own worlds. Now what? Would this spark-less marriage be their destiny? Having made it this far, now what would they do? Would they just throw in the towel or somehow suck it up and endure?

I Quit

"I quit." Have you ever said those words? Of course, we all have at one time or another. Perhaps it was at the twenty-first mile of a marathon. Your legs were like rubber, and you had nothing left to give. The expression that is often used is "I hit the wall." It is that point when you are convinced that there is not an ounce of energy left to keep you going.

Maybe it was that job that you stayed at until there wasn't another day left in you. Your supervisor was arrogant and critical, and he pontificated about every subject imaginable. No matter what you did, it never seemed to be good enough. You were passed over for promotions because you were working diligently while a less-qualified person was "kissing up" to the boss. Finally, that Friday afternoon came when you were convinced you couldn't take it anymore and you boldly announced, "I quit."

There are any number of situations where we have found ourselves ready to resign, and sometimes that may be very appropriate. But what happens if you resign your job emotionally? "What?" you may ask. What happens in the workplace if you decide within yourself that you have had it and you are done, yet you don't actually quit your job? In other words, you have given up on the hope of the job ever getting better and being a satisfying place to work; yet because you still need the paycheck, you stay. Oftentimes I find that individuals attempting to live in this dual state within their jobs become stressed, anxious, and depressed. They may cease to be productive and contribute little to the team.

In exploring the definition of the word *resign*, I came across the following meanings that are relevant to our discussion: "to submit; yield; to resign before the inevitable; to submit oneself without resistance." It can even carry the idea of giving up or signing over control to another.[2] Some of these definitions actually summarize the feelings many spouses have about their marriage. We may conclude that the hopelessness of the situation with which we are faced is inevitable. And if that is truly the case, why bother to resist? So, we might find ourselves willing to give up control of whatever the issue may be just to be left alone: "All I want is peace, and if resignation will get me that, sign me up." Unfortunately, what we call "peace" is not peace at all. Peace requires proactive engagement, and typically, at this place of resignation, engagement is the last thing on our minds. We are actually willing to settle for something that is simply a lack of conflict, a cessation of hostilities. And most are willing to give up a great deal in order to avoid conflict.

When my oldest son served in the army, he was deployed for a year to Iraq. While there, he worked as a rear gunner and he conducted "overwatch surveillance" on a convoy detail. He rode in the last vehicle of the detail with his head out of the top of it as he watched for those who would attack them. This was a dangerous task as it was not uncommon for the enemy to fire at them. However, he would be the first to tell you that just because no one shot at them on a particular day, that in no way meant that they had achieved peace. They simply had not been forced to engage in conflict.

In our marriages we are hoping for more than a lack of conflict. When we said, "I do" on our wedding day, we were looking for something greater than just getting through our week without having our spouse taking emotional shots at us. We desired a proactive, fully engaged "peace." As the months and years unfolded with untold conflict, we eventually said, "I quit. I'm not doing this anymore. I am no longer going to take emotional risks with this person who has become the enemy."

In war, when the enemy evaluates the situation and determines that defeat is inevitable, they usually withdraw their forces before they suffer greater loss. In doing so, they may leave a void, an absence that creates danger and vulnerability for the people of the country. We have seen that happen in many international conflicts.

Our marriages are no different. As we emotionally resign, give up, and withdraw from this person to whom we committed our life, we leave ourselves and our spouse vulnerable—vulnerable to loneliness, vulnerable to stress, vulnerable to heartbreak, and vulnerable to the attention and affections of another.

We can choose to "quit" our marriage in a couple of ways. One is when we choose to throw in the towel. We see no hope, no chance for improvement, so we pull the plug. We say, "I give up. I can't do this anymore. I want a divorce."

The other way we can resign is to choose to endure. In other words, rather than deciding to leave and divorce our mate, we make a conscious choice to stay. Sometimes people who do this view themselves as victims or martyrs who put up with being unloved and mistreated. They may see themselves as sacrificing their happiness for the greater good—for the sake of the kids, to keep the parents happy, to maintain an image, or for financial reasons.

But what happens when we resign from engagement and choose to just endure? In choosing to simply endure, how relationally vulnerable do we make ourselves?

No Respecter of Fame or Wealth

In July 1981, the world witnessed a storybook wedding that cost in excess of fifteen million dollars. Prince Charles and Princess Diana became one of the most watched and followed couples of that time. Within three years they had two sons. Life appeared to be well on its way for the Royal Family.

However, they failed to develop common interests; instead, each pursued his or her own agendas. The marriage began to show strain, but they were able to keep that from the public view for a while. However, once word of problems leaked out, the press had a field day. The couple spoke to the press through friends, each blaming the other for their marital struggles. Diana reported that Charles was unsupportive and insensitive to her needs. He stated that she was needy and emotionally unstable.[3]

Yet they were in an unusual situation: they weren't just some couple living on the cul-de-sac, struggling in their marriage; they were part of the British Royal Family. They couldn't just quietly divorce and go about their lives. This would be a major scandal with all kinds of repercussions. So, they chose, at least initially, to endure.

But, as I stated earlier, choosing to endure can expose our needs and vulnerabilities, and it did with them as well. By 1986 Charles had rekindled an old romance with Camilla Parker Bowles. This relationship ripped at the fabric of Charles and Diana's marriage. Yet they continued to choose the illusion of endurance. Within a year, Diana began a five-year affair with her riding instructor, James Hewitt.[4] With the press exposing the royal couple's every move, any secrets were eventually revealed. Finally, the couple chose to divorce in August 1996.

When most of us who were alive during his presidency think of John F. Kennedy, we remember his assassination on November 22, 1963. It was one of those events that anchor you in time to where you were when you first heard the news. You may recall some of his famous quotes that were used to inspire Americans, but you may also remember that he was not known for his rock-solid marriage. Despite their marital troubles, this president and his First Lady were in the public eye and therefore could not easily walk away from one another. So, not unlike Charles and Diana, this American "royal couple" chose to endure—but not without vulnerabilities and missteps coming to light. It has been reported that the president had numerous affairs, the most famous of which was with Marilyn Monroe.

I can only imagine the impact that this must have had on Mrs. Kennedy. One article stated, "Despite her apparently laissez-faire attitude to the affair, Jackie Kennedy is believed to have suffered deep emotional pain over JFK's cheating, and his relationship with Monroe was considered the cause of much distress."[5]

As I read those words again, I think I am the most surprised at what I would consider a statement of the obvious. If my spouse was cheating on me, I would experience emotional pain and distress. If my spouse was a public figure and cheating on me with another public figure and the public was not in the dark about it, I think it would cause me "much distress" as well.

This list of public figures who have been disillusioned, have attempted to fly under the radar, and have chosen to emotionally withdraw from their spouse and yet somehow endure can go on and on. From the Clintons and other political families, to Jim Baker and other well-known religious figures, to Brad Pitt and other Hollywood celebrities—those who have initially chosen to endure have found themselves in hurting and wrecked places.

Now some might say that it is more difficult for those in the public eye to address these choices, and there is certainly some truth in that statement. However, others might also view those families as having economic advantages that would somewhat insulate them from the ramifications of such choices. Still the point is made—whether you are famous or obscure, wealthy or poor, young or old, coming face to face with a relationship that has left you discouraged is inevitable. And when that relationship is a marriage, it can be unhinging.

What to do? "I am faced with the reality that my dream is in tatters. I am in disbelief at how I got here, and no matter what I try to do, it only seems to dig the hole deeper. I try to lay low and stay out of trouble, but to no avail. I have had it. I am spent. I am ready to wave the white flag, throw in the towel—do whatever I need to do in order to get a break from the chaotic merry-go-round I am on. But divorce seems so hard. I know that it can be really tough for the kids, difficult financially, and such a disappointment to family and friends. Yet I just don't think I can go on like this. I have to do something."

"Maybe I can figure out a way to endure. Perhaps if I just hunker down, focus on what makes me happy, grit my teeth, and pursue my own agenda, that will bring me some level of satisfaction. And maybe, just maybe, that will be enough. I mean, let's face it—if I can pull that off, I will still be better off than many of my friends who are in their own dysfunctional marriages. Plus, that way I don't have to weather the stigma of a divorce. Misery or divorce—what a lousy choice to have to make."

Misery Loves Company

Yes, misery or divorce are lousy options to choose between, but there will be plenty of people who will want to influence you in one direction or the other. As a matter of fact, no matter what choice you make, there will be those who will welcome you into their existence as well as those who are upset that you chose to leave theirs. Confusing? Let me explain.

I have experienced communities of couples who have adopted dysfunction and seeming unhappiness as a way of life. When they get together, the women go off into the kitchen while the men congregate on the back deck. No problem so far. But it is the pattern of conversation that takes place in those gatherings that is concerning. The women complain about their husbands, their kids, their jobs, their church, their other friends—just about everything, it would seem. They are unhappy with their marriage and, in turn, their lives, and they "kvetch" (a great Yiddish word for "complain") non-stop.

Out on the deck, the men are similarly grumbling: "Man, all she ever does is nag me that I am not doing the things around the house that she wants." "She says that I never take her anywhere. Good grief! What does she expect of me anyway?" The other men nod in agreement about how unfairly treated they are by their wives.

When you see these couples together, they sit with their arms crossed, scowls on their faces, never touching one another, and rarely interacting with anything other than words of sarcasm, all of which, of course, serves to confirm everything about which they have been "kvetching."

It is easy to understand the phrase "misery loves company" because none of us want to be miserable by ourselves. We unwittingly endeavor to pull others down with us so that we can feel validated and supported in our own unhappiness. If I am unhappy and you are too, I don't feel quite so bad.

But what happens if you reach the breaking point and choose to divorce your spouse? I mean, surely all your friends with whom you have been commiserating will be understanding and supportive. Don't bank on it. They need for you to stay a member of their "misery club." How dare you upset the status quo and do something (good or bad) about your relationship. You have violated the marital code of "kvetching."

However, you don't need to worry too much. While this unhappy group may place a "black sheep" label on you, there is another group awaiting you with open arms. Those husbands and wives who have either initiated or been blindsided by a divorce will welcome you into their version of "club misery." They will gladly invite you to join their pursuit because they don't want to be alone in their unhappiness any more than you do.

Now I must warn you, their rush to move on, medicate their pain, and prove that they are still desirable may take you down a treacherous road. If they are numbing their pain with the weekend bar scene, with happy hours on steroids, or by glopping onto the opposite sex as quickly and as frequently as possible, be prepared for an entirely different version of misery. These behaviors may initially feel freeing, but they are likely to enslave you to a completely different level of pain and are detrimental to your long-term health.

Now I know these people are your new friends whom you believe genuinely care about you and are there for you, and that does feel reaffirming. But see what happens if you make a move toward health—whether that is reconciling with your spouse, joining a support group, or eventually moving forward into a healthy relationship. Your friends may initially express verbal support, but over time you will see that you no longer fit in the club. Misery loves company, and you are choosing to leave their particular version of misery. You won't fit in there anymore.

It is no doubt frustrating to feel that you have to be willing to choose dysfunction to fit in somewhere, whether that be with your unhappy couple friends or your wounded single friends. Both groups are chasing the wind in one form or another. And yet, we have experienced this kind of interaction with groups all our life. It is these very experiences that should drive us toward healthy relationships with intentionality.

As parents, it is clear to us that if our children start hanging out with the wrong type of crowd, they easily can become corrupted in a very short period of time. As a result, we become very protective with our children and we will watch over them closely when they are old enough to start choosing who their friends are going to be.

God has that same protective desire, as our Father, for us. And we are encouraged throughout Scripture to be wise in whom we choose to allow to influence us (Prov. 18:24; 27:9,17). For regardless of how strong you may believe yourself to be, your friends will influence you. It may be in positive ways or it may be in ways that lead you down a deteriorating path, but they will impact you.

It is for this reason that the writer of First Corinthians says, *"Do not be misled: 'Bad company corrupts good character.' Come back to your senses..."* (1 Corinthians 15:33-34). As parents, we try to communicate this warning to our kids. But when we are in a place of pain, misery, and vulnerability, we would do well to remind ourselves as adults of this very true life principle.

Just as God warns us about the dangers of aligning ourselves with those pursuing the fleeting moments under the guise of "having a good time," He also encourages us with the wisdom of healthy connections. An often-used passage in wedding ceremonies expresses the words of King Solomon recorded in Ecclesiastes:

> *Two are better than one, because they have a good return for their work: If one falls down, his friend can help him up. But pity the man who falls and has no one to help him up! Also, if two lie down together, they will keep warm. But how can one keep warm alone? Though one may be overpowered, two can defend themselves. A cord of three strands is not quickly broken* (Ecclesiastes 4:9-12).

I appreciate the practicality of this passage and its affirmation of how *"his friend can help him up"* (Ecclesiastes 4:10). I believe that is a key phrase in helping me to choose those whom I will allow to have influence in my life. Those to whom I give permission to speak into my journey need to have something of value to say. Continuous "kvetching" isn't it. Telling me that I need to do whatever makes me happy or whatever works for me doesn't cut it either. The shallowness of society's empty philosophies will not "help me up." It may feel good for the moment when I escape my heartache with the numbing assistance of a bottle (or two or three), but rest assured—it will only take me deeper into the sinkhole of misery.

Instead I am encouraged by the simple yet wise words of King Solomon again, in Proverbs 27:17: *"As iron sharpens iron, so one person sharpens another."* There is mutual benefit in the rubbing of two iron blades together: the edges become sharper, making the knives more efficient in their task of cutting and slicing. In the same manner, as I connect with individuals who understand what life is meant to be, my thinking is clarified as I gain a clearer understanding of God's desires for me. Man wasn't created to live in isolation. As we discussed in an earlier chapter, God designed people to be in relationship with each other. But these relationships should spur us on to become all that God intended.

Yes, misery loves company. However, I don't have to choose to live among the miserable. I am in control of whom I allow to speak into my life. And I choose those who will truly "help me up."

At Least I Didn't Get a Divorce

Pretense is an interesting and sometimes mildly entertaining approach to observe. I recently had a client report to me that his wife had retained an attorney and filed for a "separation." She did this because "she doesn't believe in divorce." All the components of the filing and the eventual ramifications are going to play out exactly the same as if she had filed for divorce. The splitting of finances, the sale of the family home, the decisions around child custody and visitation, and, of course, the adversarial relationship—all the same. But somehow, in her eyes, because she didn't file for divorce, she didn't violate any of her religious beliefs. The "I didn't get a divorce" picture is still intact.

Another event that can seem to preserve this image is a wedding anniversary, which can be a powerful acknowledgement of a relationship's longevity. For some it is a date that they ignore or only give lip service to. For others it is a genuine occasion for celebration. When they are milestone anniversaries such as those marking fifty or sixty years of marriage, we tend to "ooh and aah" and applaud this grand achievement. Yet for many, this achievement is less than grand.

It is far too common that I see couples celebrating (if you would call it that) their fiftieth anniversary with family and friends in a festive setting. "Yeah, what's wrong with that?" you ask. Nothing, except for the fact that they can't stand each other. They sleep in separate bedrooms, hang out in different parts of the house, don't have a kind word to say to each other, constantly talk disparagingly about each other to their friends, and despise one another most of the time. They have lived in that miserable place for forty-five of the past fifty years. Their children have experienced the tension between their parents every holiday when they are home. Their neighbors have heard the frequent earsplitting arguments and the profanity-laced conversations that they have with each other. Their friends know how miserable each has been for decades. But here we are tonight celebrating this fifty-year fiasco…oops, I mean marriage.

Everyone is dressed elegantly. The professional photographer is taking pictures of the smiling (through gritted teeth) couple, and toasts are made honoring them. But it gets confusing to watch and figure out. Just what is it are they are celebrating? Are they rejoicing in the fifty wonderful love-filled years they have had together? Absolutely not! Are they having a party to recognize the blissful partnership they have enjoyed for all this time and to acknowledge how much they are looking forward to those years that lie ahead? Of course not. Then why? Because they have endured a miserable relationship and survived. Hmm…that hardly sounds like a reason to rejoice.

It is amazing how many couples are doing this very thing. It would be like having North and South Korea throw a party because they have not yet obliterated each other from the map. They are still enemies and despise each other. There is no trust and no plan in place to make anything better. They can't stand each other. But let's throw a party and smile. I know that sounds ridiculous—and it is. However, it is no different from what many couples engage in on that "special day."

It is enlightening to listen to the spin that this toxic couple will put on their fifty years together: "Well, it hasn't always been easy"—an understatement—"but at least we didn't get a divorce. We are committed." Is that what this is all about—getting brownie points? At least we didn't get a divorce? That's kind of like the two Koreas saying, "At least we haven't blown each other up yet." Now of course, if the Koreas made that statement and followed it with "because we are committed," we would choke on our anniversary cake. Committed? Committed to what—a peaceful relationship, mutual cooperation for the benefit of all, a supportive connection that seeks the best for the other? No, a commitment not to kill each other. Really? That is what we are celebrating—the fact that for fifty years, this couple hasn't killed each other? Well, hmm…"at least they didn't get a divorce."

Years ago, I recall hearing an insightful definition of sin simply as "missing the mark." We read in the Scriptures that God cares for us, and He does so enough that He has given us pretty clear instructions by which to live. Whether we are reading the Mosaic law or the teachings of Jesus, we clearly see God leading because of His great love for us. He says that if we love Him, we will obey Him (see John 14:23). Anything other than that is "missing the mark" and is sin.

We read many places in Scripture teachings about marriage and divorce. Whether it is God declaring *"I hate divorce,"* as He does in Malachi 2:16, or Jesus's teaching in Matthew 19 concerning God's intentions for the permanence of a lifelong, healthy marriage, we clearly see that divorce is "missing the mark" (Malachi 2:16 NASB; see Matt. 19:1-12). Few who believe in the Bible would dispute that (except under certain circumstances) divorce is sin. It is for this reason that so many choose to endure a despicable marriage—so that they can proudly state, "At least I didn't get a divorce. I was committed." Another way of saying this might be, "I didn't get a divorce, and therefore I didn't sin. Instead, I was righteous and endured, which demonstrates commitment."

I hate to rattle the status-quo thinking, but here it goes: endurance does not equal commitment. Okay, let that sink in for a minute. Now I will say it again: **endurance DOES NOT equal commitment.** Yep, you heard me right. Enduring, surviving, hating but not killing each other is not the same thing as commitment. *Commitment* is an important and powerful word at which we will take a closer look in the next chapter. For now, the important thing to realize is that yes, we have been called to commitment in our marriages; however, there is more to commitment than mere forbearance. But if endurance is not commitment, then what is it? Endurance as described here is, very simply, "missing the mark." If we are called to commitment but choose to endure instead, we have missed the mark.

So, the logical question then is, "If divorce is sin but simply enduring is also sin, what's the difference? I mean, if I am going to be miserable by staying with that wretched spouse and doing so is sin, I might as well get a divorce. If I am going to sin either way, doesn't it make sense just to go ahead and get a divorce?" That is a great rational question. But before you run to the attorney and file papers, at least indulge me long enough by reading the next chapter and thinking through this very question with me.

"[A] Marriage [license] does not guarantee you will be together forever. It's only paper. It takes love, respect, trust, understanding, friendship and faith in your relationship to make it last."

—Unknown[1]

Chapter Five

Commitment–A Different Approach

It began as a warm summer day with the hint of a breeze in east Texas. Annie's Aunt Nancy, with whom she was very close, and her Uncle Jack were celebrating their fifty-fifth wedding anniversary. Doug and Annie had traveled to Tyler, Texas, to be a part of this event. It was a very special day that they did not want to miss.

During their drive, though, they both found themselves deep in thought. Here they were, making a trip to see a couple that was going to be recognized by family and friends for their lengthy yet successful marriage. While Doug and Annie were genuinely happy for them, they also couldn't help but reflect, each to themselves, upon their disappointment with their own marriage. The had been married twenty-eight years, and their marriage felt like a prison in so many ways. Yet here they were, on their way to see a couple who had been married almost twice that long. The thought of another twenty-seven years together with the way things were cast an unspoken gloom over Doug and Annie. They could both feel it, and it was stifling.

Arriving at her aunt and uncle's was a joyous reunion. Annie's parents and siblings were there. Neighbors whom Annie hadn't seen since she was a child were excited to see her as well. Annie's family, who were well aware of the struggles that she and Doug had encountered over the years, tended to be a bit standoffish with Doug. While he attempted to make polite conversation, it felt forced and uncomfortable. So, he found himself slinking off into the corner, trying to become as inconspicuous as possible.

The party was pleasant. A string quartet played in the background. The pastor from Nancy and Jack's church led the couple in a renewal of vows that was actually quite moving. Friends shared stories of their experiences with Nancy and Jack over the years. Songs were sung, and toasts were made. Then it was the couple's turn to speak.

Doug envied how happy Annie's aunt and uncle were. They truly seemed to enjoy each other's company; they appeared to have what Doug had hoped for. This couple had been lifelong role models for Annie, and she was thrilled at their love, even though she hadn't been able to obtain that for herself.

What happened next was more than unexpected. Jack stood up and made a toast to his bride that brought tears to Annie's eyes. Then he began a story. He spoke of the early years of their marriage that had not always been easy. He talked about how complacency had eroded their relationship to the point that they found themselves leading very separate lives. Once the kids (Annie's cousins) had grown and moved away, Jack and Nancy discovered that they were living with strangers. Fearful about and depressed by how they envisioned this future together, they had actually contemplated divorce.

Annie was stunned by this unexpected revelation. The times that she had spent with her aunt and uncle had always seemed pleasant. But she now realized that she had, of course, always seen their relationship through a kid's eyes.

Doug was riveted by Jack's story—probably because it was Doug's story too. He wondered how they had managed to endure. But for Doug and Annie, this narrative they were hearing continued to parallel their own journey in unimaginable ways.

Jack went on to share how he and Nancy had retreated into their individual lives with feelings of abandonment and either unspoken bitterness or harshly spoken resentment. They had a choice to make: Would they go ahead and divorce or would they figure out a way to endure? After all, they had thirty years invested in the marriage, and they hated the thought of how a divorce would impact their kids, grandkids, family, friends, and church community. Yet at the same time, the thought of simply enduring what had become a "roommate existence" was equally unappealing.

Doug was beginning to wonder if this was some kind of a set-up to expose his and Annie's relationship because it all sounded eerily familiar.

Nancy joined in the storytelling and said, "It was about this time that I was having coffee with one of my girlfriends. I laid out for her my gloomy dilemma—divorce or endure this life-draining relationship? I was miserable and needed help with the decision. I was caught off guard when my girlfriend responded with, 'Why are those your only two choices?' I didn't understand. What other choices were there? My girlfriend asked, 'Why isn't there a third possibility—being committed and reengaging in your marriage?'"

"I was thoroughly confused. I mean, we were committed—we hadn't filed for divorce. But she went on to suggest that what we were living was not commitment."

Annie squirmed at was she was hearing. This was hitting way too close to home.

Jack and Nancy took turns telling their story of how, over a period of time, they began to approach their marriage differently, beginning to look at it through the eyes of commitment. Via a number of avenues—seeing a marriage therapist, attending a couple's retreat, and even reading books and praying together—they began a process of re-infusing life into their nearly dead relationship. As the heart monitor of their partnership began to sound a healthy, rhythmic beat, life took on a different feel. Spending time together became something to which they looked forward. Trips were anticipated with excitement instead of dread. And it was a pleasant surprise one day when they both realized that they were spending their life with their lover and best friend.

It hadn't happened overnight, nor had it been easy. Jack had to learn to love all over again. Nancy had to become intentional about the flavor of her conversation. Then Jack cautiously began to lower his walls of emotional protection, and Nancy waded into trusting again. They had both worked diligently to rescue their marriage.

Where were they now? Jack proudly proclaimed that for nearly twenty-five years, he had been privileged to journey toward this anniversary with the love of his life. With tears of joy, Nancy expressed her unwavering commitment to this man without whom she could not imagine living.

While Jack and Nancy embraced to people's applause, Doug looked at Annie, wondering…just wondering…

Choosing

"Decay is normal. In the natural process of aging, machinery wears out, buildings fall into disrepair, pictures fade, and our bodies lose their tone and strength. Scientists say, in fact, that everything in the universe is perpetually moving to greater and greater disorder—a state of entropy. You don't have to be a quantum physicist to know that even the most beautifully designed and well-built house will eventually crumble if left unattended."[2] I appreciate this statement by Gary and Barb Rosberg because it is such an important principle in marriage that is so often overlooked.

I know the necessity of changing the oil in my car or tightening a loose hinge on my front door. In order to keep things working well, proper maintenance and repair are critical. But not only are they necessary for my lawnmower or my car; they are essential to my marriage. If I don't address them there, I will be facing that question we discussed earlier: Do I divorce or endure? Unfortunately, my marriage is not like a self-cleaning oven. It is not designed to take care of itself. I have to choose to care for it. And the best way that I do that is to choose commitment.

The word *commitment* conjures up a number of thoughts for people. For some it is a straitjacket, of which we may think when we talk about a violent person being "committed." Others prefer to think about commitment in terms of a particular level of involvement. Still other definitions include "pledge," "obligation," "promise," or even "engagement."[3] I am particularly drawn to other aspects that include the ideas of "giv[ing] in trust" or "hand[ing] over for safe-keeping."

Commitment can certainly include a promise and a level of involvement, but part of the reason we struggle with this issue so much is due to the fact that what we often experience as "commitment" is missing the "safe" part. When I commit myself to my wife, I am certainly making a pledge that I will engage with her, but I am also trusting her with myself. I am giving myself to her for safe-keeping. But what happens if she isn't to be trusted? What if she won't safely keep me? There is the rub. According to Gay and Kathlyn Hendricks, "A co-committed relationship is one in which two… people support each other in being whole, complete individuals."[4]

Yet this level of engagement is often not supported by societal trends. A strong case for this is made by Tim Keller when he says, "Marriage used to be a public institution for the common good, and now is a private arrangement for the satisfaction of the individuals. Marriage used to be about *us*, but now it is about *me*." He elaborates on this by stating, "But ironically, this newer view of marriage actually puts a crushing burden of expectation on marriage and on spouses in a way that more traditional understandings never did. And it leaves us desperately trapped between both unrealistic longings for *and* terrible fears about marriage."[5]

In the twenty-first century, words like *obligation* and *commitment* are seen as restrictive words. They cramp one's expression, style, and perhaps one's personality, and they are not in vogue. Society is much quicker to embrace ideas of "freedom" and "liberation." Anything that limits your ability to "pursue your dreams," or to "make yourself happy" is seen as oppressive. Ideas such as honoring a promise, demonstrating responsibility, and being accountable in your relationships are not valued. As a matter of fact, there is a relentless pursuit to cast aside those things or people that society would view as "hindering your growth as an individual." Yet as Keller goes on to say, "It is the newer view that has led to a steep decline in marriage and to an oppressive sense of hopelessness with regard to it."[6]

Many years ago I had a golden retriever named Rocky. I had moved onto an acreage that was not fenced in. You would think that this would have been a prime opportunity for Rocky to take off and run until I could catch him. However, it actually had the opposite effect. He would go out the front door and wait for me. The openness without boundaries created fear and insecurity in him. Here he had all this room and freedom to run and instead he remained close by, uncertain of where it was safe to go.

However, once I fenced in the property and he had the chance to explore it, he approached his surroundings very differently. He learned that he could go anywhere he wanted to and there was a perimeter that offered safety. Stray dogs and other animals could not get to him, and he didn't have to worry about fast-moving cars or school buses. He was safe. And with that safety came freedom.

While I was at work during the day, I would leave Rocky in his dog run, which was connected to the house and was a smaller area in which he could stay. Once, during a snowstorm, I left him with food and water in the garage instead. Unbeknown to me, when I left that morning, blowing snow caused the garage door opener sensor to trip and reopen the door that I thought was closed. Because I had left him in the garage, I didn't bother to close the property gate.

When I arrived home that afternoon and saw the garage door open, I feared the worst. I began to imagine where he might have gone. I was scared that he had wandered onto the main road that was heavily trafficked. My mind was panicking as I imagined all kinds of unhappy endings. How surprised I was to find him lying in the garage as I pulled up. He had never left. Now one would, of course, like to think that he was like Lassie from the 1960s television series and that he was way too smart to leave, or that he instinctively knew that I would be displeased and that it was the wrong thing to do—that is, of course, unless Timmy fell in the well; then it would be okay to go rescue him. (If you are not old enough to have seen the show, forget that last sentence.) We all want our dogs to be that brilliant. However, that was not the case. He was in the garage, nervous and uncertain. But once the gate was closed, all was well again and he knew he was free to run, chase rabbits, and bark at everything.

Similarly, it is this very concept of commitment between two individuals that gives them freedom. My wife and I don't see the vows that we have declared to each other and have chosen to honor as holding us back. Exactly the opposite. It is because I know that she loves me not only when I am healthy, but even when I am sick with the flu that I know freedom. Being able to trust that I will love her when she looks and acts her worst as well as when she is at her best likewise gives her comfort and security.

When we were married, the minister gave us a gold three-stranded cord. One of these strands represents my love for her, while another pictures her love for me. I am glad that we have those two strands because one by itself would easily snap. But it is the third strand that truly gives the cord its strength. That additional strand signifies the essential role that God occupies in our life. Ecclesiastes 4:12 says it this way: *"...A cord of three strands is not quickly broken."* Now I know this may sound cheesy, but it is true; just ask my wife: we keep that cord on our nightstand, and about once a week, we pull on our respective ends to remind us that the knot is tight and representative of our unbreakable commitment to each other.

Do we feel caged or stifled? Absolutely not. The more we grow in our commitment, the more freedom we experience. The more we are willing to acknowledge the independence and interdependence in our relationship, the stronger our bond and the greater our security. She knows that I will be there when the dust settles. I, in turn, know that she will be there in all the uncertainty that lies ahead.

Choosing Frequently

One of the reasons that we keep that reminder of the three-stranded cord is because commitment is not just something we do on our wedding day and then ignore it. Making a commitment is something we do every day. I mean, on day two or three of your honeymoon you may not have felt the need to make verbal renewals. But by week two, when you learn that he throws his stinky socks on the floor or that she leaves her makeup all over the bathroom counter, the need for daily reminders of your commitment to your spouse may begin to emerge. Of course, for anyone married a few years, you know that the challenges to your marital vows become much, much bigger than just those kinds of issues. Whether it is due to issues of money, in-laws, intimacy, parenting, or even chores, the foundation for your lifelong promise can be eroded. Most everyone experiences doubt and dark periods in their marriage. Yet it is our commitment to our spouse that can help to see us through these tunnels. As we discussed earlier, commitment is easy when all is well. It can be incredibly difficult when life is not going the way we had envisioned.

For some, commitment is regarded as boring. One author described that perception as feeling as though it's "just about staying in a marriage until you die."[7] Wow, that does sound boring. I want nothing to do with that. However, that idea couldn't be further from the truth. Commitment is actually the framework that allows vibrancy to safely grow in your relationship. It is the structure that creates confidence and security. It is the boundary that encourages us to run free.

I recently came across a story shared by author Linda Bloom. She had some friends who were intentional in their decision to celebrate their commitment to each other. Rather than take an approach of "How long will this marriage last?" they chose to create and build a strong history of commitment throughout their marriage. The manner in which they did this was quite inspiring:

> When he got married, he enjoyed his wedding day so much that he said to his wife, "We should do this every year!" And they have, seventeen times. They have gotten married in many different traditions: by a Baptist minister in the French West Indies; in an Anglican ceremony in England; by the skiing judge in Vail, Colorado; by a kahuna on the beach in Hawaii. Once they got married on shipboard by an Episcopalian minister sailor; they had a Buddhist ceremony at the San Francisco Zen Center; and one year, Al Huang, a tai chi master, married them in a ceremony at the Esalen Institute in Big Sur, California. A Mexican judge once married them in Cabo San Lucas with a mariachi band playing, and the next year they got married near Tucson by a Navaho elder

who brought his family in native garb to bear witness to the ceremony.[8]

Now I am not suggesting that you have to travel to faraway places at great expense to recreate ceremonies in elaborate settings. It isn't necessary for you to discover your "inner free spirit" and engage in traditions that "are not you." That is not at all the point of this story. Rather, it is to encourage you with this principle of commitment. It is to demonstrate that commitment should not be something that has grown stale and lies covered in cobwebs. It can be exciting, creative, vibrant, refreshing, invigorating, and life-giving. It can infuse your marriage with fun, hope, security, interdependence, and freedom. As a matter of fact, I want to suggest that if what you believe is "commitment" in your marriage has grown lifeless and stale, it is not commitment at all—but endurance.

In this decision point of "divorce or endure," endurance, as we have been discussing it, is actually the antithesis of commitment. Commitment is rejuvenating, while endurance is deteriorating. Commitment creates life; endurance drains us of life. Commitment sets us up with a trajectory of hope, while endurance is a resignation to hopelessness.

Big Picture

Recently a friend of mine suffered a broken tooth. He had simply bitten down on a piece of steak, when "crack" went the tooth. In relating the story, he said, "Yeah, the dentist warned me this could happen. He said that I could have the problem repaired for a couple hundred dollars or I could wait and take the chance that more damage could occur. Now I am looking at a possible root canal and crown. I guess I should have listened. It's just that when he told me that, I didn't want to spend the money. I guess I shouldn't have just looked at the moment."

Many of us have found ourselves in countless situations where we could take a short-term look or we could take the long view and look at the big picture. Sometimes focusing on the moment—such as taking my hand off a hot pan—is important to do. However, at other times it can wind up resulting in a situation like the tooth. If we are only considering how we feel right this minute, we might quit our job, tell off the policeman, eat the entire half-gallon of ice cream, or scream at our spouse and file for divorce. All those decisions may lead to bitter regret later on.

However, when we consider things through the "big-picture lens," our decisions may be tempered with more consideration given to the outcomes. Commitment enables us to take that long view of our marriage. It allows us to put the daily ups and downs of our partnership in perspective. This, in turn, helps us to react less impulsively, assisting us in making more thoughtful decisions.

Now I recognize that what I have just described is easier said than done, perhaps especially for our Baby Boomer generation, of which I am a part. Mark O'Connell expresses this understanding when he says that we are:

> Products of a 'we can have it all and if we don't somebody is to blame' culture, we hold tight to our already overextended adolescences. We imagine that all gratifications are possible, that all losses are avoidable, and that all constraints are negotiable. As a result, we experience life's hardships and complexities as unnecessary inconveniences rather than defining, meaning-making aspects of being human.[9]

He is accurate in the fact that we don't want "hard." We want "easy" in our schooling, in our jobs, and especially in our relationships. However, we just as clearly know that life doesn't operate that way. Just ask those who are on a professional sports team or those who have designed and constructed architectural marvels. These endeavors require patience and stick-to-itiveness. It is absurd to expect that the most important relationship in our life should require no less.

In a conversation between Jesus and the religious leaders of the day, as recorded in Matthew 19, the subjects of marriage and divorce were being discussed. The leaders were caught in a conflict of understanding regarding two different Jewish schools of thought about when divorce was appropriate. One, the Shammai school, contended, based on a passage in Deuteronomy 24:1, that husbands could divorce their wives for basically any reason that they wanted. However, the Hillel school took a quite different position, maintaining that divorce could happen only if there had been adultery. After they present this question to Jesus, He begins to teach them, saying *"Haven't you read...that at the beginning the Creator 'made them male and female,' and said, 'For this reason a man will leave his father and mother and be united to his wife, and the two will become one flesh'? So they are no longer two, but one flesh. Therefore what God has joined together, let* [man not] *separate"* (Matthew 19:4-6). As His disciples heard this, even they thought that this sounded difficult—to honor a commitment to one's spouse for life. Like most of us, they wanted the option of an exit plan. This teaching seemed awfully demanding.

Yet is it? As we have discussed earlier, couples want safety and security; they want to be exposed but still valued—or as we called it, "fully known and fully loved." I am convinced that, when all is said and done, people who marry truly want to know that this person with whom they are beginning a new life will still be there at the end when the dust settles. At the core of our existence, we long for the very thing God has designed—a relationship that oozes with commitment and that is anchored in such a way that we know our mate is not going anywhere. Many may be hesitant to make that guarantee, but most all of us desire it from our husband- or wife-to-be. As Scott Stanley says, "The problem is not with the vision; it's with the fact that it's hard to attain."[10] My response to that is yes, it can be.

So, I guess the question with which we are faced is whether or not this idea of commitment is worth it.

Previously in this chapter I mentioned that in the early days of our culture, marriage was seen not merely as a private matter between two individuals, but also as a public institution with implications for the greater community. If that is the case, who is impacted by my decision? Who gains or loses as a result of my choice to divorce, endure, or commit? While there may be a variety of answers to that question, for our purposes I will just mention a few who are affected: children, parents, friends, neighbors, the church community, and most importantly, the two married individuals. I recognize that there are some horrific circumstances when divorce may be called for and all those impacted are much better off for that decision. I would contend, though, that those situations may be rare and that most people, including the couple, experience a much fuller and richer life when they pursue a commitment approach.

When we choose to endure rather than addressing our disappointments in a meaningful way, our relationships drift apart and our dreams fade. As this happens, Gary D. Chapman writes, "we dam up the stream of life and tend to create a stagnant pool of self-pity. We feel alone because we are alone. We may still live in the same house, but we live as two lonely people rather than as a unit."[11] And when this happens, we very possibly will miss God's best.

A Picture

But what does God's best look like? That is hard to say, as God's best may look very different for couples in how it plays out. But I am confident of this: His best includes security and hope.

I am a visual person. I will understand when you verbally explain something to me—that is, of course, unless it is something along the lines of calculus; then all bets are off. But when you show me a picture, I will understand even more clearly. I want to share with you one picture of what commitment looked like for a couple.

For twenty-two years Robertson McQuilkin was president of Columbia Bible College and Seminary in South Carolina. He traveled extensively as a speaker as well. But he made the decision to walk away from the ministry that he loved in order take care of his wife of forty-two years when she was diagnosed with Alzheimer's disease. While it is clear in his book *A Promise Kept* that his world quickly changed from one of well-known leadership to one in which he fed, bathed, and took care of all his wife's needs full-time, it is also important to know that this decision was motivated by his deep love for his wife Muriel.

Some encouraged him to institutionalize his wife, but that was not a decision he was inclined to make. As a matter of fact, in announcing his resignation, he said:

> The decision was made, in a way, 42 years ago when I promised to care for Muriel "in sickness and in health… till death do us part." So, as I told the students and faculty, as a man of my word, integrity has something to do with it. But so does fairness. She has cared for me fully and sacrificially all these years; if I cared for her for the next 40 years I would not be out of her debt.[12]

Robertson recounted a letter he once read that had been sent to a national columnist that told of how a person had ended a relationship because it wasn't meeting that person's needs:

> The counselor's response was predictable: "What were your needs that didn't get met by her in the relationship? Do you still have these needs? What would she have to do to fill these needs? Could she do it?" Needs for communication, understanding, affirmation, common interests, sexual fulfillment—the list goes on. If the needs are not met, split.[13]

He went on to say, "There is an eerie irrelevance to every one of those criteria for me."[14]

One time a women asked him about the difficulties of caring for his wife:

> "Don't you ever get tired?"
>
> "Tired? Every night. That's why I go to bed."
>
> "No, I mean tired of…" and she tilted her head toward Muriel, who sat silently in her wheelchair, her vacant eyes saying, "No one at home just now."
>
> "Why, no, I don't get tired," I responded. "I love to care for her. She's my precious."[15]

He also relates his experience of receiving a letter from his friend recommending that he discontinue his role as caretaker:

> "Muriel doesn't know you anymore, doesn't know anything, really, so it's time to put her in a nursing home and get on with life." The day may come when, because of a change in my health or hers, she could be better cared for by others. But for now she needs me and I need her.
>
> I responded, "Do you realize how lonely I would be without her?"[16]

> Another time, during the earlier days of Muriel's illness, they had a flight delay in the Atlanta airport. Waiting with her for a couple of hours was no easy task.
>
> Every few minutes, the same questions, the same answers about what we're doing here, when are we going home? And every few minutes we'd take a fast-paced walk down the terminal in earnest search of—what?…
>
> An attractive woman executive type sat across from us, working diligently on her computer. Once, when we

returned from an excursion, she said something, without looking up from her papers. Since no one else was nearby I assumed she had spoken to me or at least mumbled in protest of our constant activity.

"Pardon?" I asked.

"Oh," she said, "I was just asking myself, 'Will I ever find a man to love me like that?'"[17]

What a clear picture Robertson gives us of commitment. Yes, his was an extreme situation, but one that any of us could encounter. There is no doubt that this man was committed to his spouse. And isn't the businesswoman's question one that we all would ask for ourselves? "Will I ever find a man [or woman] to love me like that?" I want that—don't you?

So...What Now?

In our journey so far together we have revisited the ideals for marriage. We have recalled our disillusionment, discovering that it was maybe not all that it was cracked up to be. Thinking back on our attempts at solving problems by "flying under the radar" has reminded us of how empty and unproductive that avoidance mechanism has been. Learning that endurance does not equal commitment has forced us to admit that simply enduring did not achieve the utopia we thought would experience if we didn't divorce. But now we have come smack-dab face to face with God's call for commitment. Perhaps you recognize that in a perfect world, this might have merit, but you are fearful of another crash-and-burn experience. You don't know that you can handle more disappointment. You understand the benefits if commitment works, but you have no idea where to begin.

Up to now, the purpose of the book has been to bring you to this point of understanding that God absolutely wants to bless you in your marriage. And that begins with commitment. Grasping His purpose for you will enable you to begin to make desperately needed changes. The remainder of this book will be geared toward helping you begin those needed steps. I hope that you will stay with me as we discover a different approach.

"Your soulmate is not someone who comes into your life peacefully. It is [one] who comes to make you question things, who changes your reality, somebody that marks a before and after in your life. It is not the human being everyone has idealized, but an ordinary person, who manages to revolutionize your world in a second."

—Anonymous[1]

Chapter Six

Lessons From Success–Engagement

What a confusing time! Doug and Annie drove back from east Texas still reeling from the revelation that her aunt and uncle had experienced marital struggles that so paralleled their own. While they didn't talk much, their minds were both spinning at warp speed, trying to reconcile their preconceived version of their relative's marriage with the new reality into which they had been given a peek.

What had they missed? Where had they taken a wrong turn? How had their own marital dream decayed into this nightmare? Each of them had read books that discussed the contributors to marital strife. Finances, sex, children, in-laws—they were both masters at identifying problems. As a matter of fact, when it came to recognizing the flaws in each other, they were like master copy editors, each spotting the minutest of mistakes.

When she met with her friends, Annie would listen intently as they shared similar crash-and-burn stories. For their part, Doug and the guys would grumble without ceasing about what things were not working in their marriages. They all seemed to have it down pat. They had figured out where all the problems and blunders were in their spousal relationships—or so they thought. Without a doubt, they knew how to do it wrong. They had learned the lessons of failure.

Yet knowing how to achieve some level of success had eluded them. The possibilities associated with success had not been part of their discussions. They only talked about what they knew—failure. And somehow, they found a comfort in this strange familiarity, this same-sex kvetching.

One Friday afternoon, Doug left work early to meet with their financial planner, Dan, regarding some of their investment goals. As Dan politely inquired about Annie, Doug inadvertently found himself suddenly spewing the same kind of marital toxins that he usually saved for his buddies. Dan remained quiet and thoughtful as Doug emptied his frustrations. Finally, Dan asked the following question: "Why do you come to me for advice?"

"What?" Doug asked, clearly caught off guard.

"Why do you come in here to meet with me? Oh, I know we have been friends for decades, but why do you come in here to discuss finances? Why don't you go find a fund manager who has been losing his client's money with regularity?"

"Are you nuts?" Doug replied. "That doesn't make any sense."

"But," Dan continued, "that fund manager is probably an expert at what doesn't work. He knows all the strategies that have failed."

"Why would I want that?" Doug replied. "I come to you because you have been successful in managing my money. I come to you because you know what works."

"Exactly!" said Dan. Dan had his attention now. "Do you know how people in the banking industry learn to spot counterfeit money?"

Doug thought for a moment and said, "I guess they study all the things that look bogus."

"That seems like a logical thought, Doug, but in reality, they do the exact opposite. They study legitimate dollars in such detail that they can spot a fraudulent bill in a heartbeat."

"Okay, but I am not sure I see your point," Doug stated.

"My point is this: you know all the components that lead to failure in your marriage. You have studied them all too well. But why not try a different approach, one that has worked well for you financially? Why not study the aspects of marriage that have proven successful for couples? Why not study what works?"

This seemed so obvious. It was embarrassing that he hadn't seen this before. He looked at Dan and simply said, "Thank you for that advice. I think I need to try that." Then, with a smile and a wave of his hand, he said, "See, I knew there was a reason I came to see you today."

Success Isn't Always Easy

My guess is that you haven't picked up this book because you've found marriage to be easy. While there may have been some highlights, you likely are reading this now as a result of relentless links in what feels like an unending chain of difficulty. It would be Pollyannaish if I were to gather stories from couples who have sailed along with few issues. Certainly some of those narratives exist, but I doubt that you would take solace in them or gain any degree of hope.

But what if there were stories of success from real people who have encountered real struggles—maybe even some of the same challenges you are facing? Would that possibly be of value?

For this chapter I have interviewed four different couples. All of them are in lengthy marriages, and all of them have had obstacles to overcome—some of them pretty steep. These couples were gracious enough to grant me extended time for meeting with them in their homes, where they openly recalled their years of marriage. In order to protect their privacy, names have been changed and some details of their circumstances have been slightly altered. In each case, the individuals interviewed consented to give me a window into their journeys for the sole purpose of assisting you, the reader. These marriages of twenty-nine, thirty-four, thirty-eight, and forty-seven years were achieved with intentionality, but not always easily. Each couple is grateful that they have reached this season in their marriage and believe themselves blessed to have done so. They offer to you whatever you might glean that could benefit your current situation. Their desire is that you would be able to experience the joy of marriage that they have come to know. Understand that in each case, there were times of reservation, doubt, struggle, and in some cases separation and decisions to divorce. Yet, ultimately, they chose a different path—one that changed the trajectory of their future. And they are glad that they did.

Don and Marissa

Although they had grown up in nearby towns and had attended neighboring high schools, they had never known each other. It was not until the age of thirty-two that they met. Don was not where he had expected to be at that point in life. His wife had died some time earlier, and he was doing the best that he could as the single parent of a two-year-old. He met Marissa at church and, after four dates, proposed. They just seemed to know that they were a fit for each other, and their friends were supportive of the match.

Paralleling the speed at which the relationship had developed was the quick transition to which the marriage was forced to adapt. Don's parents lived with him, with his mother providing needed assistance in raising his two-year-old son. Just a few months before, Marissa had been a carefree single adult. With her marriage to Don she was suddenly thrust into the roles of wife, mother, and daughter-in-law. Navigating these roles successfully was quite a challenge, especially when she felt as though her mother-in-law was constantly looking over her shoulder passing judgment on her parenting skills.

This arrangement continued for about a year, at which time Don's parents moved into their own place. Yet, with hardly a break for the newlyweds, Marissa's mother moved in with them for health reasons and lived with the family for twenty years. When asked how they dealt with this stress, they stated three things: first, they continually prayed about their circumstances; second, they worked to be as sensitive as possible to all people involved and affected; finally, they made a clear decision to persevere and do what they needed to do to make their marriage work.

Their determination was evident when Don made the statement that at one point, because of the ongoing focus on her mother's needs, he began to feel that Marissa needed to make a choice—"either me or her." As he spoke in the interview about the ultimatum he never voiced, Marissa was surprised. She had never known that he felt this way, as he had never told her. They "did what they needed to do."

One of the most challenging seasons of their marriage was when they moved to Detroit for his job transfer. Between the bleak gray skies of the city, their inability to conceive their own child, and their emotional struggle with being rejected as adoptive parents, Don went into a deep depression. He would sometimes go sit on the bed with the lights out for extended periods of time. Despite her best efforts to understand how these circumstances were affecting him, Marissa was at a loss. She hadn't a clue as to how she could help him.

Fortunately, they learned three valuable lessons through this dark season. First of all, they each have strengths as well as weaknesses. Compensating for the struggles of the other is essential to functioning as partners, as a team. Second, they talk to each other. Neither is too proud to say, "I need your help." They do their best not to hold back or bottle up feelings. And lastly, always reminding themselves and each other of their faith in the Lord continues to provide them with the strength that they need to face any situation. While that may sound like some spiritual salve, it is actually anything but. It is an intentional choice in how they walk and live in the daily grind of life.

Larry and Linda

"Hey Blondie, I sure would like to be your Dagwood," were the words shouted from the school bus to Linda. She coolly ignored his obvious pickup line. But when this high school junior got onto the bus, all the students had conveniently arranged themselves so that the only seat remaining was next to him—Larry, a senior. It wasn't long before they became sweethearts at this Air Force base high school, and three years later they were married.

Growing up as military children, they had a saying: "If we don't move after three years, we will have to clean the baseboards." The fact that Larry had attended four different high schools accurately reflected this mantra. But this continual propensity to transfer and move would actually prove to be great preparation for their future life together.

The first three or four years of their marriage were probably the most challenging for them. Following the completion of college, Larry went to work for a major oil company, resulting in many moves and lots of travel. Upon arrival in a new country, he would quickly be immersed in the hustle and bustle of the job. However, Linda would often find herself isolated as a stay-at-home mom. Linda related the difficulties of weeks spent in a hotel room with little knowledge of the language in the country in which she would find herself.

The challenges of living abroad were amplified when their girls returned to the United States to attend college. Knowing that they couldn't just respond to a phone call by hopping into the car made the overseas gap feel even greater. This distance contributed to a whole set of stressors.

I appreciated two strategies in particular that they used to help each other adapt to their new surroundings. First, they would unpack all their boxes as soon as they were able and say, "This is home." Not all families would do this. Some would leave things in boxes, viewing their new location as temporary, but certainly not home. However, doing so would have slowed their ability to embrace their new surroundings. Secondly, whatever country they found themselves in, they quickly involved themselves in a local church. Making this connection and becoming a part of a faith community went a long way toward helping them to adapt and settle in. They emphasized the essential nature of those people connections—people to share their lives with, people to pray with them and for them, and people who cared.

Parenting was an issue that could have been a major dividing point for them. Due to the frequency of Larry's travels, Linda functioned a large percentage of the time as a single parent. As therefore might be expected, when Larry was home, he tended to be lenient, while Linda had to serve as more of the disciplinarian. Although their parenting styles were quite different, they were committed to respecting each other's position and working to be united in their dealings with their children. This proved successful.

Nathan and Emily

Lying about her age in order to land a job in the office supply store had worked. Emily, not quite sixteen, had impressed Nathan, who hired her into their family business. He thought, "Wow, not only is she attractive, but she has a great personality." Approximately a year and half later they were married.

But even before they got to this point, they were nearly derailed. Nathan had convinced her that she could trust him around sex and that he wouldn't get her pregnant. Yet the first time they had intercourse, she got pregnant. She was young, disillusioned, and scared. She couldn't tell her parents and got an abortion. This part of the interview was a difficult, tearful conversation for her. She lost trust in Nathan, and they didn't speak for well over a month. Eventually they began to talk again, but scars had been created and trust did not return quickly.

From the beginning of the marriage, it was a struggle. They had great difficulty understanding each other. Neither had good role models to show them what marriage should look like. Along with a several year age difference, they came from different cultures and different faiths. Nathan's dad was, as he described him, "an Archie Bunker type." As a result, Nathan did not treat Emily well. He would explode at her in anger and then frequently would leave to get away from the house. This pattern of distance continued for nearly a year and a half. As he stated, he would "booze it up at night," abusing both alcohol and drugs. He viewed himself as a generally happy guy, but with a short fuse, blowing up at anything and anybody. It was almost like he was looking for a reason to get mad. Emily did not see this side of him while they were dating, as he had been a perfect gentleman. But once they got married the façade came down.

Emily had moved to this country at the age of ten. Describing her home as "loud and chaotic," she was actually a quiet, low-key kid. While she loved Nathan, she also loved the idea of marriage and saw Nathan as her ticket out of the chaos. You can imagine her dismay when the loud and explosive side of Nathan erupted.

On top of this were some stark faith differences. Emily had been raised Catholic. She had no idea that God was relational and only saw Him as sitting in judgment of her. But she had gone through confirmation as a child. On the other hand, Nathan was Jewish, and Emily's parents had some strong negative preconceived ideas about Jewish people. It was a real struggle for her family.

As I listened to their story, I was anxious to learn what had enabled them to make it to this snowy day in November nearly three decades later. How had they pulled this thing out of a seemingly irrecoverable tailspin?

First, after a year and a half of her husband drinking, using drugs, and being emotionally absent, Emily sat Nathan down and issued an ultimatum. This could not continue. She was ready to be done and leave. He had to change or she was gone. Her direct approach got his attention. It forced him to take a long, hard look at why he was drinking, at why he was needing to fill his life with alcohol and partying. He often would say that he "needed to go out and have a good time." He knew there was a void but didn't know what it was caused by.

Interestingly, at about this same time, his secretary of nine years told him that she was going to resign because she couldn't watch him destroy his life. Even though she had been talking to him for years about God's desire for his life, it was as though he was hearing the gospel message for the first time. He accepted the Messiah as his Savior that night. Nathan realized that he had been abusing alcohol and partying in an effort to fill a void that only the God of the universe could fill. The trajectory of his life and their marriage began to change that very night. A new journey was launched as they both started to understand the loving, relational nature of God and His grace in forgiving their sins by the sending of His Son.

The second step they took was to embrace counseling. They have become strong believers in seeking the assistance of wise counsel at needed seasons of their life. Whether it was learning better ways to deal with anger, techniques for addressing differences in parenting styles, or ideas for overcoming the challenges of PMS, they knew what they didn't know and sought help in those areas. This has been significant and beneficial. As Emily said, "We don't know it all—we are still learning." Accessing help at needed times has been priceless.

Brady and Stephanie

It was twenty-two years into what seemed like a rock-solid marriage that things began to fall apart. Brady had a prestigious career and was steadily climbing toward the top of his field. Unfortunately, what came with his position of power was a sense of ego and pride that went to his head and that ultimately was his undoing. He had a short-lived affair. One's first thoughts at seeing "short-lived" might be, "Well, that's not so bad. At least it wasn't a long and involved one." But Brady would tell you that it cost him a career that he dearly loved. "It was scandalous and horrible," he said, going on to note that he "lost his life." Stephanie would echo that.

His was a slide that has consumed so many. Women found him attractive, and he didn't resist their advances. Stephanie added that she "had no idea" and that he was the last one that any of their friends would have ever imagined doing this. He looked good on the surface. But in his ego, he would rationalize, "This is harmless. Who could it hurt? I can stop at any time." Looking back, he now says that this kind of reckless choice and its lasting damage "can happen just like that." No one is immune from the consequences of this kind of tumble.

Brady began to meet with a pastor for six months. Stephanie was not sure that she could get past this so she made a very intentional choice to find a woman to meet with who had experienced being cheated on but who had managed to work through it and remain married. It was important for her to connect with someone who had found successful strategies for working through these intense issues.

As Brady continued to do all the right things, Stephanie forgave him, and they lived happily ever after. Well, not exactly. It was only a few years later when Brady cheated again. This time it was not a short-lived relationship but one of twenty-two months. It was with a woman who even had been in their home. And it was the other woman who finally told Stephanie what was going on.

Lessons From Success—Engagement

Up to this point, they had hidden the previous affair from their families. Imagine the hurt that Stephanie experienced as their families lavished sympathy on Brady, supporting him while they believed he was being unfairly maligned in his career. All the while, Stephanie knew the truth, and she was dying on the inside. After the revelation of this second affair, they came clean with their families.

As you read this account, with your blood pressure slowly rising, you may be saying aloud, "Kick the bum out!" In essence, that is what Stephanie did. They separated, with her clear intention being to divorce him. She was done!

But then, over the next year and a half a slow transformation began. Brady was in weekly counseling, fully believing that his marriage was over, and had become actively involved in a small men's accountability group. He knew this was essential if he were ever to become a transparent man of integrity. Stephanie was in counseling too, primarily to figure out how to move on with her life. Yet whenever she contemplated moving forward with the divorce, she just couldn't seem to find peace. She knew logically that she was more than justified, but in spite of it all, she still loved Brady. However, being in that relationship just couldn't be healthy. Finally, after expressing her dilemma to her pastor, she received the following advice: "If you are not going to divorce him, then the only other reasonable choice is to consider reconciliation." This scared her beyond measure. But the seed was planted.

Brady and Stephanie started going to marriage counseling, and eventually she moved back in—but only in a "sister-like" relationship. During this time, he voluntarily submitted to a lie detector test. This enabled them to begin a slow and arduous climb back to life. Brady was totally broken, believing that he had lost Stephanie as well as his children. Up to now he absolutely believed that she was never coming back.

Over time, trust was slowly rebuilt. In one of our meetings, Brady stated that "because of what I did and the fact that she has remained married to me, this has led me to love her at a depth I can't describe." He explained, "She is my best friend and my wisest counsel. She always gives me perspective. My heart has been softened, and my eyes have been opened to what I have. And my loyalty and commitment are forever." Wisely, to this day, Brady is actively involved with other men in accountability groups and touts, with fervor, their benefits. He has learned that when we are able to hide behind a mask of "having it together," it is all too easy to fool ourselves as well as those around us. As the deception becomes an ingrained pattern of living, destruction of the person and the family is just a small step away. Brady and Stephanie came about as close as a couple can come to being done. But by the grace of God and a commitment to each other, they have been married for over thirty-eight years.

Insights

These four couples are just four couples. But they are clear representations of struggles that so many have encountered. Perhaps you can relate to some of their circumstances. Others reading this might be wrestling with issues that haven't been discussed here, such as addictions or criminal activity. But whatever you may be facing, I encourage you to listen closely to the tips and insights that these couples share. These individuals do not offer platitudes that come from a smooth ride. Their suggestions come as a result of having been in the muck of the trenches and learning what worked and discovering what steps they wish they had taken to avoid so many difficulties.

While the complete list of interview questions will appear in the appendix, I want to examine and summarize these couples' answers to two important questions here.

1) What factors, have you learned, are the most important for a vibrant marriage?

Lessons From Success–Engagement

- Communicate. Talk to each other—at a heart level. Don't stuff your feelings.

- Diligently work to "out-love" the other person.

- Strive to always give honor and respect to the other.

- Never say anything derogatory in public about your partner. If you say anything at all, make sure that it is positive.

- Set joint standards about money and live within your means.

- Share joint finances.

- Be willing to compromise and do your best to see each other's viewpoint.

- Make a commitment for the long haul. (These couples know that is not always easy.)

- Never go to sleep in separate beds because you are angry with each other.

- It is essential to have a common faith. God is the center of vibrancy. As Nathan stated without hesitation, "If we hadn't discovered God and put Him at the core of our marriage, we would have fallen apart."

- Pray together.

- Commit yourselves to being united when facing difficult situations.

- Give each other the freedom to fulfill what God has called each person to do.

- Be each other's biggest and loudest cheerleader.

- Be accountable to trusted same-sex friends with whom you can bare your soul.

- Continually offer forgiveness.

- Don't wait until a crisis to get help. Seek godly counsel.

- Learn each other's love language and get fluent at speaking it.

- Be intentional in moving from simple independence to greater interdependence.

- Honor (even when you don't understand) the things that are important to each other.

- Commit to having no secrets from one another. Be honest and transparent.

- Learn to be best friends.

- Determine and commit to each other not to walk away.

- Be humble.

- Never fool yourself into thinking that you can't fail and blow it—because any of us can.

- Don't get complacent. Keep dating.

- Find good marital mentoring.

2) What tips would you give to couples who are feeling stuck and without hope?

- Go back and retrace your steps that led to your "stuckness."

Lessons From Success–Engagement

- Find the things that you did not deal with back when you should have and begin to address them.

- If making the kids a priority over your spouse has led to where you are now, ask your mate for forgiveness.

- Don't work to change your spouse. Work to change yourself!

- If chasing after money has contributed to your problems, stop. Learn to be satisfied with what you have.

- Seek out strong Christian counseling. This has been essential to many couples in getting "unstuck."

- Commit yourselves to regular "tune-ups," such as an annual marriage retreat. Couples who actively pursue these kinds of events are much healthier than couples who only venture there when their marriage is in shambles.

- Join a couples Bible study group where you can journey and grow together.

- Be deliberate in planning weekends and trips.

- Begin to pray together. (This make take some time and might happen only after some level of trust has been re-established.)

- Don't settle for getting into a rut.

- Build "guardrails" of protection around your marriage.

- Communicate with each other about where you are stuck and why (e.g., sex, finances, kids, priorities, etc.).

I very much appreciated the thoughts and insights that these couples shared. Their advice came out of hard-fought struggles and is battle-tested. As a result, their words have the power that comes with both suffering and success. I am deeply grateful for each of these couples, their stories, and their wisdom.

As I wrapped up the interviews, I asked each couple if there was anything else they wanted me to know. Larry and Linda's words were revealing when they said, "We have learned not to argue over petty things but to focus on things that have eternal value—namely, God and our relationships. We have learned how important the family unit is to the health of our society. We do not want to get to our deathbed and have regrets of not spending more time with our family. It is overwhelmingly important that we make the most of each day, stay the course, and finish well."

"Let your faith be bigger than your fear."
—Francis Chan[1]

Chapter Seven

The Critical Puzzle Piece

Annie's head was spinning. She had appreciated her Aunt Nancy's well-intended suggestion that she talk with some of her friends who seemed to be happier than she and Doug were. However, with each conversation, she came away with more ideas than her head could contain. One of her girlfriends was convinced that vacations were the reason for the success of her own marriage. Another recommended a wide variety of books on marriage that had helped them. Still another explained valuable communication tools that she and her husband had learned from their therapist. And Annie must have received at least another dozen suggestions from other friends.

While all the advice seemed to have merit, she didn't know how to sort it all out or where to begin. In trying to make some kind of sense out of it, she was beginning to feel almost as despondent as she had when she began this quest to acquire tips from friends.

Following through on their agreed-upon quest was even more of a challenge for Doug. Talking with his guy friends was easy—as long as the conversation was around their three F's: fishing, football, or fast cars. But the added fourth "F"—feelings—was extremely uncomfortable. He tried to approach his buddies, who seemed to get along decently with their wives, in hopes of learning their secrets. But some of the guys looked at him like he had three heads, while others seemed clueless as to what it was he was asking. He began to regret having ever brought up the subject.

One Saturday morning, he and his best friend Cliff met for coffee. Observantly, Cliff commented, "Doug, you seem agitated this morning. You okay?" That was all the opening Doug needed. He launched into a narrative of what had been going on—from the celebration of Annie's aunt and uncle's anniversary to their joint pursuit to discover the secrets of a happy and successful marriage. Cliff inquired as to what Doug had learned so far. "Oh man," he said. "I have heard it all—from just saying, 'Yes, dear' to whatever she wants, to bringing her flowers every week, to making date night a priority. Not that all the suggestions are bad, but it just seems like there ought to be more—something more significant."

As he paused, Cliff asked him, "What is the most foundational piece to any of this?"

"Ah—love," Doug responded, thinking that sounded like a proper and politically correct answer.

"Hmm…perhaps in a manner of speaking," Cliff replied. "Let me ask the question a little differently: Why are you here? Are you just on a mud ball randomly flying through space or is something more purposeful going on here?"

Suddenly Doug felt as though he were about to embark on a conversational journey from which he would not return quite the same. And he was correct. Cliff was about to challenge Doug's thinking in a way that would rattle and potentially stretch his and Annie's frame of reference beyond their comfort zone. But maybe a shifting paradigm was exactly what they needed.

The Puzzle of Your Life

Have you ever sat with your spouse, kids, or other family member and attempted to work one of those five-million-piece puzzles? Okay, perhaps it was only 500 or 1,000 pieces, but it sure felt like more than that. Oftentimes the picture is of some crazy thing like a cloud or lake or something else where every piece looks the same. Yet, as you get into it, you begin to notice the slight differences in colors and pieces and begin to get some clusters put together. Finally, after three or four years (another possible exaggeration—or not), you complete the puzzle, only to find a piece missing. And if, by some chance, it happens to all be there, then you want to glue the finished product to a board and hang it on the wall because it took a major chunk of time to complete it. At least that is what I want to do. But for some reason my wife never wants a picture of a cloud or giraffes hanging on our wall so it all goes back in the box to be worked on again one rainy day.

Our lives can often be viewed as a puzzle. Different pieces represent various aspects of our life—there is the education piece; the one that is our family of origin; friends; hobbies; spouse; children; career; and the list goes on. While some individuals appear to have hundreds of complicated puzzle pieces, others seem to be a less cluttered picture. But regardless of which one we have, I am convinced that, like that five-hundred-piece puzzle, only certain pieces fit in certain spots. If you are like me, you have probably found a piece that almost fits while working on the puzzle. "If this one side just curved a little bit more to the right, it would be a perfect fit." But the reality is it is not a perfect fit. In my impatience, I may try to force the piece in or I may want to get the scissors and do a trim job to make it fit, but the truth is, it doesn't fit. If I force it, the picture ultimately will not work.

Oh, how very much this picture applies to our lives! I see this in many individuals: when a single mom relates to her only child in an almost substitute spousal role; when a career becomes a person's complete identity; or when the rise or fall of someone's favorite sports team makes or breaks his weekend. Whatever the situation, forcing a puzzle piece where it does not belong can cause damage and create emptiness. I see this most clearly demonstrated in marriage.

Scripture convinces me that we are each created with a variety of needs. There is no question that we were created with a need for a companion, as we have read in Genesis, as well as a need for meaningful work (see Gen. 2:18). We have a need for rest and a need to parent and love our children. These are all significant needs and should never be minimized. However, the one puzzle piece that we often relegate to the bottom of the box is our need for God. From the very beginning, we see that man's strength, his fulfillment, his very existence is, first and foremost, dependent upon God. Without God, life becomes *"a chasing after the wind"* (Ecclesiastes 1:14).

A few years ago I encountered a client who was frustrated as a result of the struggles in her relationship quest. She was constantly trying to remake herself and find significance within herself. I remember her telling me that she had a wall in one room of her house that was covered in quotes that she had gathered from a variety of sources. Every time she would find some new saying that had to do with finding happiness and inner peace and pulling oneself up by one's own strength and determination, she would tack it up. And yet, here she was in tears as we talked about the relational happiness and peace that she so desperately wanted but did not have.

I began to talk with her about this differently shaped puzzle piece that only God can fill in our lives. Her strong recoil surprised me. If you were desperate for peace, wouldn't you want to explore the core reasons that you are lacking it? She absolutely did not want to go there. She did not want to seek out the Creator of the universe who knows her better than she knows herself. "I have to find happiness and contentment within myself before I can include God in the picture," she said. Wow—that is kind of like saying, "I have to get the car started first and then I will put gas in the tank." Without the source of strength and purpose at the core of my existence, I will continue to be frustrated. But she was bent on filling that God-shaped piece with her own strength, pursuits, and relationships.

Frequently, individuals find themselves frustrated in their marital relationship because they similarly attempt to force the right piece into the wrong place in the puzzle. I appreciate the way that Tim Keller states this: "If I look to my marriage to fill the God-sized spiritual vacuum in my heart, I will not be in a position to serve my spouse. Only God can fill a God-sized hole. Until God has the proper place in my life, I will always be complaining that my spouse is not loving me well enough, not respecting me enough, not supporting me enough."[2]

I want to look briefly at a few examples of those who have determined to fill that God-shaped hole with something other than Him.

We Will Create Our Own God

We are a generation that desires instant gratification. However, this is not new. Humankind has always been impatient, as is clearly seen in Exodus 32. In the account that is reported here, we see that Moses had gone up on Mount Sinai to receive the Law from God. He was there for forty days, which stretched the waiting ability of the Hebrew people. When they had concluded that they just couldn't wait on him any longer, they demanded of Aaron, Moses's brother, that he make an idol for them that would be their god. Caving in to their demands, Aaron collected gold earrings that the people were wearing and melted and fashioned them into a golden calf. These people had been rescued from Egypt by God and miraculously led through the Red Sea to their destination. They had seen the awesome power of God Almighty. Yet, as unbelievable as it seems after all that they had witnessed, here they were, in their impatience, willing to create their own god and bow down to a metal idol.

The short version of the story is that when Moses returned, there was utter chaos in the camp. Moses drew a clear line in the sand for people to choose between God and their own creation. As a result, approximately 3,000 people who were determined to worship a god of their own making lost their lives that day (see Exod. 32:1-35).

I wonder how many of us have created our own version of a golden calf, someone or something that rules our life? It doesn't matter how much notoriety we receive or what we accomplish in the eyes of the world. If we choose the wrong idol, it can be deadly.

I recall reading in early 2014 about the death of Philip Seymour Hoffman. He was an acclaimed actor and talented director who seemingly had the world at his fingertips. Yet his drug and alcohol addiction could not fill the void. He was found on February 2, 2014, with a needle in his arm, dead from "acute mixed drug intoxication, including heroin, cocaine, benzodiazepines and amphetamine.[3] What a sad and unnecessary loss.

My Significant Other Can Meet All My Needs

I remember a conversation I had many years ago with a relative who was a single mom. She had begun dating a man for whom she cared a great deal; however, the relationship had hit a bump. He wanted her full attention even though she had custody of her two young children. One day he gave her an ultimatum—him or the kids. At face value, most of us would think that an easy decision. However, it didn't seem so simple to her, and she shipped her kids off to live with their dad. She had chosen the man. Like all of us, she had the God-sized hole in her life, but rather than allow Him to fill it, she chose a relationship. She was determined to force this puzzle piece to fit where it obviously didn't.

Many have heard the story of Samson and Delilah as recorded in the Book of Judges. But what some may not realize is that this is a story of choices. From before Samson was born, we are told in

Scripture that *"no razor may be used on his head, because the boy is to be a Nazirite, set apart to God from birth, and he will begin the deliverance of Israel from the hands of the Philistines"* (see Judges 13:5). By honoring this vow, he would be given great strength by God.

We read that Samson was attracted to a Philistine woman, one of the very people from whom he was to free Israel. His parents tried to convince him to marry someone from his own people, but like a child throwing a tantrum, he would not be consoled. He had to have her. He was convinced she could fill the void and meet his every need. As the account continues, we find that not only was this not the case, but his marriage to her led to him killing over a thousand men, and his wife was given to another man. God had given Samson incredible strength for him to use in leading the nation of Israel. But so far he was simply using it to protect himself from the messy predicaments he was creating.

Some time later, Samson fell in love with a woman named Delilah. She was trouble from the start, as she conspired with the Philistines to destroy him. Delilah needed to know the source of Samson's great physical strength. He initially refused to tell her. However, she persisted in nagging him day after day. She whined that if he really loved her, then he would confide in her and tell her his secret. I can only imagine the emotional threats and ultimatums that she gave him if he didn't reveal the mystery of his strength to her. This woman, this relationship became so important to Samson that he was willing to betray his nation. He was looking to her to fill the vacuum that only God can fill, and in doing so, he turned his back on God. As a result, he lost his God-given strength, he lost his freedom, he lost his ability to serve his people, and he lost his life.

I Need What They Have in Order to Be Happy

When I was 5 years old, my mother always told me that happiness was the key to life. When I went to school, they asked me what I wanted to be when I grew up. I wrote down 'happy'. They told me I didn't understand the assignment, and I told them they didn't understand life.[4]

Oh the things that we do in the name of happiness. We see the toys that another kid has, and we have to have them. We get them, only to find that they don't make us happy either, so we go after the next kid's toys; and the pattern continues. Then we grow up—or one would hope. But if our fulfillment is found in keeping up with the Joneses, then the pattern really does continue. They get the new pool and so we do too. They win the award for best lawn in the neighborhood so we add more fertilizer to ours.

During the time that the prophet Samuel was a judge over Israel, the elders came to him and asked him to select for them a king. They sounded like us as children (or adults) when they said, *"Now appoint a king to lead us, such as all the other nations have"* (1 Samuel 8:5). Samuel is disappointed in their request, but God's response to him is, *"Listen to all that the people are saying to you; it is not you they have rejected, but they have rejected Me as their King. As they have done from the day I brought them up out of Egypt until this day, forsaking Me and serving other gods, so they are doing to you"* (1 Samuel 8:7-8). Samuel warns the people that they are not going to get what they bargained for. He lets them know what to expect from the rule of an earthly king. But they don't care. All the other kids have the newest Transformer toy, and they want one too.

It isn't long in their history before they realize that a king was not such a great idea, but by then it is too late. I find God's response to Samuel—when He says that they are not rejecting Samuel; they are rejecting God—to be so apropos. You see, when we chase after puzzle pieces that are shinier or seem to have brighter colors and try to force them where they don't fit, the picture is never quite right.

The Critical Puzzle Piece

Pride and Power

El Paso County in Colorado experienced an interesting power play between the commissioners and the sheriff in 2014. The sheriff was under investigation for sexual and financial improprieties and was asked to step down. He boldly refused, setting the stage for a battle. Partially in response to this scenario, the state began to look at term limits for sheriffs. Weld County Sheriff John Cooke recalls advice he was given nearly twelve years earlier when he took office: "'People have a tendency to get a big head,' Cooke said recently as he recalled the advice. 'Don't do it. Just because you're elected and people want to talk to you doesn't mean you're anything special.'"[5]

We live in a world where power is valued. Whether it be as president of the country or head of a department in a school district, people like to be in charge. And so often that desire to be in control leads to pride and just plain stupid decisions.

One such example is recorded in the Book of Daniel. Nebuchadnezzar, who was king of Babylon, had allowed his power to go to his head. He decided to have a golden image made that was ninety feet high and nine feet wide. The Scripture says that he then invited governors, treasurers, judges, provincial officials—in other words, all the important people—to come together for the dedication of the image (see Dan. 3:1-3). So far so good. I suppose this was not much different than dedicating a city park or a new fire station. But now it takes an ugly turn. The king proclaims that as soon as the horn is blown, everyone must fall down and worship the image that the king had set up (see Dan. 3:4-5). Okay, now this sounds a bit radical, but he is not done. Daniel 3:6 states, *"Whoever does not fall down and worship will immediately be thrown into a blazing furnace."* As controversial as many of our government leaders have been, I haven't heard them threaten to throw me into a furnace—at least not yet.

At this time there were some who were looking for reasons to cause problems for the Jews. They reported to the king that they had noticed three Jewish men in his administration who had not bowed down to the image when the horn was sounded—Shadrach, Meshach, and Abednego. This would have been a great time for the king to realize that his demand might be a little whacky. But no, he is royally angry instead. He calls the three men before him, reminds them of the order, and gives them another opportunity to bow down, thinking himself reasonable. He warns them that if they don't prostrate themselves before it, no god can save them from him (see Dan. 3:13-15). One would have hoped that somewhere along the way the king would have recognized that his head had way exceeded his hat size and that maybe his pride had gotten of control.

I love the response of these three men. "[They] *replied to the king, 'O Nebuchadnezzar, we do not need to defend ourselves before you in this matter. If we are thrown into the blazing furnace, the God we serve is able to save us from it, and He will rescue us from your hand, O king. But even if he does not, we want you to know, O king, that we will not serve your gods or worship the image of gold you have set up*" (Daniel 3:16-18).

Hmm…that is a pretty bold proclamation on their part. These three men knew with certainty that God could save them. But even if He chose not to, they were sold out to Him completely and would serve no other but Him. I think that would have caused me to pause and reflect on what I was doing, but not so for the king. He had the blaze cranked up on the furnace, and the three were thrown into the fire. As a matter of fact, the fire was so hot that the soldiers throwing them in were killed by the fire (see Dan. 3:19,22-23). What happened next shocked the king. The passage says that he "[jumped] *to his feet in amazement… He said, 'Look! I see four men walking around in the fire, unbound and unharmed, and the fourth looks like a son of the gods'*" (Daniel 3:24-25).

On the one hand, you have a power-crazed king who is finding new ways to exert his control—and yet, even these attempts don't fill the emptiness inside—while on the other hand, you have three men who confidently know who is in control. They have embraced the only puzzle piece that will fit in that God-shaped hole—God. And their very souls are satisfied.

Riches and Stuff

In 1988, Pennsylvania lottery winner William "Bud" Post found himself $16.2 million richer. However, within a year he was $1 million in debt. He stated that winning the lottery was a nightmare and that he wished it had never happened.[6] An article in *Business Insider* explains that:

> a former girlfriend successfully sued him for a share of his winnings and his brother was arrested for hiring a hit man to kill him in the hopes he'd inherit a share of the winnings.
>
> After sinking money into various family businesses, Post sank into debt and spent time in jail for firing a gun over the head of a bill collector.
>
> Bud now lives quietly on $450 a month and food stamps.[7]

In Luke 12:13-21, Jesus tells the story of a rich man whose field produced a tremendous crop. He began to ponder what he would do with all his riches and decided he would tear down his barns and build bigger ones. In other words, he needed more storage for all his stuff. He said to himself:

> *You have plenty of [good things] laid up for many years. Take life easy; eat, drink, and be merry.' But God said to him, 'You fool! This very night your life will be demanded from you. Then who will get what you have prepared for yourself?' 'This is how it will be with [anyone who] stores up things for [himself] but is not rich toward God* (Luke 12:19-21).

It doesn't matter whether we are the rich man in the story or the lottery winner in Pennsylvania—money and stuff are puzzle pieces.

There is nothing wrong with them, but again, if we attempt to fill our desperate need for God with financial security, we will surely find that the void—our need for a source of strength greater than anything this world has to offer, our need for a Redeemer of our lives—still exists.

We could continue to look at countless narratives: the son in Luke 15 who wanted his complete freedom because he thought that would make his life perfect when in fact it nearly destroyed him, Simon the sorcerer in Acts 8 who tried to buy the power of God, or King Saul, whose disobedience to God and jealous pursuit of David in First Samuel 23 drove him to a place of overwhelming misery (see Luke 15:11-32; Acts 8:9-25; 1 Samuel 23:7-29). Without fail, trying to do life without allowing the Creator to fill His designated place leaves us in pursuit—pursuit of the perfect job, the perfect body, the perfect relationship, the perfect _____. You fill in the blank.

The Puzzle Piece Impacts How I Am as a Married Person

Whether or not I have God in His rightful place in my life definitely impacts how I am as a married person. I mentioned in the first chapter that most often in a marriage ceremony, there are two sets of vows—one set that I make to God regarding my spouse and another that I make to my spouse. In other words, there are both horizontal as well as vertical vows. And it is these vertical vows to an unchanging God that help anchor me and my marriage to something stronger than the whims and emotions of my day.

Change is inevitable. Over the course of my marriage, I will change, as will my wife. Therefore, it is important to be aware of the fact that when we make vows, they are not only promises about today, but they are mutual promises of our future love. I am declaring that I will love this person whom I have never met (because he or she is likely to change in ways I never imagined).

Now you may ask, "How in the world can I do that?" I would answer: in part because I am anchored to an unchanging God who gives me the strength, ability, and wisdom to be able to do that. But perhaps an even more important factor is that God is to sit on the throne of your life as well as your spouse's. And when that happens, change can be exciting. Not only am I committed to my own personal growth, I am also committed to seeing my spouse through God's eyes. As we do that, we are able to play a role in helping each other in our journey to become more like God and more of who He wants us to be.

So, while this chapter is not meant to be one on apologetics regarding a faith in God, it is intended to encourage you to at least begin to ask some soul-searching questions: Am I just on a mud ball flying through space or was I put here with a purpose? If the throne of my heart is designed as a place for God to inhabit, am I willing to allow that or will I keep trying to force other puzzle pieces into that hole?

While I am not saying that you must address this issue or you will never have a satisfying marriage, I am saying that it is a foundational piece that has implications for all the other pieces of your puzzle. Yes, I know there are couples whose relationship seems to work even though they have never acknowledged God. I also know far too many couples who proclaim a faith whose marriages are disasters. One could argue that simply declaring verbally that God is a priority doesn't make it so. Acknowledging that there is a piece in the puzzle that only He can fill does not fill it. It requires inviting Him in and allowing Him to fill it. When that happens—when we begin a relationship with Him—foundations with eternal significance are laid and the opportunity for magnificent change in our life, including our marriage, becomes available to us.

When God Almighty is given a place of preeminence in our life, redemption of all the other puzzle pieces can commence. And I would contend that the size and significance of our entire puzzle picture changes. I appreciate the fact that Scripture says that He is the same yesterday, today, and forever (see Heb. 13:8). Because He alone gives my journey—marriage, career, kids, joys, and struggles—purpose.

In 2013, the movie *Home Run* was released. It tells the fictional story of a professional baseball player named Cory Brand. He is an arrogant star who is forced into a rehabilitation program after several alcohol-related incidents. He is even responsible for injuring his brother in a drinking and driving accident. Cory is also coerced into taking on the coaching duties of a Little League team. It is only after he gets honest about his addictions and his checkered past that he begins to find new hope.

Cory had been doing his best to use his fame, addictions, and money to fill the void in his life. But, as is usually the case, he found only momentary relief at best. The God-shaped void still existed. As he began to get his head around this concept, he spoke to his addiction support group and bared his soul in the following way:

> I've used alcohol my entire life to replace the love and attention I never received from my father. But every drop of alcohol, every one-night stand will never replace the ache inside of me, an ache that only God can fill. I tried to change, but I failed every time; and I know now that I'm powerless without God. But with His help I've found a freedom from my pain and my habits that I never thought was possible. And my family has suffered for generations. And I suffer because of my father's pain, and my father suffered because of his father's pain. But this is how it changes; this is where it changes. And today I begin a new story. I'm a child of God, and I have a Father

who loves me on and off the baseball field. Thank you for letting me share.[8]

I hope that you will consider the impact that this puzzle piece can have on your life. I pray that this is how and where it changes for you and that you will begin a new story. As Cory confessed, you are a child of God and you have a Father who loves you.

"It's not the absence of conflict that determines the health of my relationships. It's knowing how to handle the conflicts that inevitably arise."
—Lysa TerKeurst[1]

Chapter Eight

Wild Blue Yonder

"This feels like Splash Mountain at Disneyland," Annie exclaimed. Doug knew exactly what she meant. She had never been a fan of roller coasters or up-and-down-movement kinds of rides. Doug remembered, with a smile, their trip a few years earlier to the theme park. He had somehow managed to convince Annie to ride Splash Mountain, assuring her that it wouldn't be that bad. Following a small chute in the course of the ride, she was inclined to agree—because she thought the drop they had just passed was the long, high chute she had seen from the outside. She thought she had survived. However, as they began to climb toward the ultimate splash, panicked, she hollered, "What is this?" He didn't have the heart to tell her. He just said, "Hang on. You'll be fine."

Yes, she was fine, but you wouldn't know it from the picture that was snapped automatically on the way down—because you can't find her in it. She was scrunched down behind Doug with her eyes closed.

She was proclaiming that their marriage felt like this theme park ride. In the course of their relationship, they had gone from the initial excitement of the ride to lazily drifting through the gently flowing waters, to navigating unexpected dips and bumps along the way, to finally dropping with fear to what they were convinced would be the ultimate demise of their relationship.

It had been a few months since Doug's conversation with Cliff. That encounter had revealed to Doug the huge, essential missing puzzle piece in his life. It had driven him to take a personal inventory and to begin to examine his life through a different lens. He started to see the ways he had endeavored to fill the God-shaped void in his life with any and everything except God. It was no wonder that he was so dissatisfied with Annie—he was dissatisfied with himself. He recognized that if he and Annie were to have any chance at all, he would have to find this first and most important piece in his life puzzle.

Annie began to notice small changes in Doug's responses to her and in his attitude in general. She just figured it was some phase and didn't put much stock in it. However, one Saturday afternoon, as she arrived home from shoe shopping, she found Doug mopping the kitchen floor. At first she figured he must have broken a dish or spilled something. But when she inquired, he responded with, "No, nothing spilled. I just noticed it needed to be mopped, and I knew how busy you had been all week." Lightheaded, she sat in the nearest chair. In all their years of marriage, Doug had NEVER done this. "What was going on?" she wondered. "Was this some head game he was playing? Was he trying to throw her off balance? Was this some hidden agenda or wicked scheme he hatched to finally 'get her'?"

It was an agenda, but it wasn't hidden. It was a plan to begin to learn how to genuinely love his wife. However, he readily admitted to her that while that was his goal, he had no idea what he was doing.

They sat for hours that afternoon, cautiously opening their minds while closely guarding their hearts. Doug shared with her his conversation with Cliff and the road that it had taken him down to rediscover the core ingredient that he needed before all others—his dependence on the God of the universe who alone could redeem his train-wrecked life, and with it, his lifeless marriage. With tears streaking her face, Annie listened. God had been nudging her with similar convictions, but she hadn't felt safe to discuss them. But now what? Dare she trust that there really was hope for something different or was she better off running in the other direction? Was this Splash Mountain playing out in real life?

In the ensuing days, there was more discussion and even a few moments of emotional tenderness. But it was still very scary. Very unnerving! Was it worth taking the chance? If so, what was the next step? How could they begin to untangle this mess? Was there any life left buried under the carnage of their history?

On the Radar

In chapter three we looked at the tactics we use to avoid detection when we feel that our mate is set on our demise. We likened these strategies to a plane flying under the radar in order to keep the enemy from shooting it down. Whether we are talking about a missile, a civilian aircraft, or a relationship, it is possible to fly under the radar. We do this by going under the "line of sight." Without this "the path of the beam is blocked" and radars are unable to "see" an object.[2]

However, I want to suggest a different approach. It makes perfect sense to not want to be seen when we are in a dangerous adversarial relationship. But what about in a marriage? I know, for many of you that has been one and the same. But what about a marriage that could be phenomenal if we came at it in a completely different manner?

We spent the first portion of this book tracking the spiral of our marriages to their dismal resting places. It didn't take a lot of effort to get there. As a matter of fact, the lack of effort may have hastened the deterioration of our relationships, which in turn caused us to become disillusioned and to attempt to withdraw to seemingly safer places. However, this led us to a crossroads: "Do I simply endure this miserable existence or do I get a divorce?" But then we began to consider a different approach. It became clear that simply enduring could be as destructive to our marriage, and to each of us individually, as the terminating process of divorce. And so with that came the exploration of commitment, an approach that takes a big-picture view as opposed to a short-term, momentary-unhappiness perspective. This then opens the door to intimate possibilities that could be enticing.

So far in the second half of this book, we have looked at some lessons from couples who have successfully engaged in the long haul. We also tackled the importance of laying a firm foundation for our marriages. I am reminded of the illustration that Jesus uses in Matthew 7:24-27, where He tells the story of two men who built houses. To describe it in contemporary terms, one man built his house with concrete footings and a concrete foundation while the other one built his wood floor directly on the sand. While both houses may have looked outwardly appealing at the onset, it was a very different story after bad weather hit. The account says that the rains, wind, and floods all came (see Matt. 7:25). We don't need to be rocket scientists to know what happened. The house with the concrete foundation stood solid even after the flood, while the house built on the sand was gone (see Matt. 7:25-27).

As we examined in the last chapter, recognizing that the Creator and Redeemer of our very existence is the foundation of our lives and our marriage is the first step toward doing this marital journey differently.

The second step is the opposite of withdrawing, hiding, and flying under the radar. It is endeavoring to stay visible on the scope, exposed (I know that sounds scary), and in the "line of sight." And I am suggesting that we begin to do that with the principles of intentionality, vulnerability, and honesty. Let's examine these three components of visibility.

Intentionality

Doing something with intention or purpose requires effort. Conversely, when we operate without intention, often little is accomplished. For example, as I look out my office window right now, I see that my lawn needs mowing. I can observe it and ponder mowing it all day long. But until I actually go out, put gasoline in the mower, and do it, the grass will only get taller and more unsightly.....

I can't tell you the number of people I speak with who have these kinds of thoughts bouncing around in their heads. They haven't told their spouse that they love them in months. Words of appreciation have gone unexpressed. They will admit to me that they have thought about it a few times. Yet if these thoughts are to become words that make a difference, these people will have to intentionally speak them. Until they do, their lack of intention (not expressing love and appreciation) will have a greater impact.

Past Hurts

> Most of us arrive at our adult relationships with a backlog of ancient hurts, fears, and angers. The source of these wounds has often been forgotten, so that it looks like our current relationships are causing us to hurt. In fact, our current relationships are the area in which we have the opportunity to clear up and free ourselves of these patterns from the past.[3]

These words ring true in the lives of most of us. We all enter our marriages with a truckload of relational junk. For those who were raised in more functional families, there may be a healthy history of connections and fewer negative patterns. However, for far too many of us, our families represented the height of dysfunction. Those unhealthy ways of relating then carried over into how we managed our interactions with others outside of our family, oftentimes in polarized ways. For example, if you were raised by a parent who was overly critical and demeaning, the result might be that you approach your own familial relationships with the same harshness and scrutiny. On the other hand, you may strongly react to the manner in which you were raised by manifesting an inability to be confrontational in the healthiest of ways. Out of fear of possibly hurting somebody's feelings, you are not able to set even the most basic of boundaries. This in turn leads to feelings of becoming a doormat for others—and you deeply resent it.

These patterns of relating, good or bad, are carried into our significant relationships. Our fears, insecurities, resentments—they all go with us wherever we go. If, as I was growing up, every time I walked through the door my dad gave me a disapproving scowl, and following that "look" came a two-hour lecture about what an irresponsible kid I was, a pattern likely took root. Fast-forward—I'm married; I come home, walk through the front door, and there sits my spouse with that same disapproving scowl. My mind races to what I know (or at least what I think I know) is coming next—a two-hour lecture about what an irresponsible husband or wife I am. Fearing that, I hurry to the basement to hole up for the evening. As all this happens, my spouse wonders why I am avoiding her and what she has done that has made me mad. She, in turn, is upset because I have avoided her so she hides out in the bedroom with hurt feelings. Oh, and by the way, that scowl that I saw on her face—it was an expression of frustration she felt as she was watching the news about the latest government financial fiasco. It had nothing to do with me. Yet it will be two days before we talk again. Wow—what a waste.

I recently sat with a couple who are living this kind of a pattern. Lately, issues of physical intimacy have been a topic of concern. Follow this scenario: The husband is relating how unloved he is and how his wife does not find him physically attractive. Caught off guard, she states that just the other day as they were getting ready for work, she had commented about what a good-looking guy he is. Without responding to her comment, he remarks, "Well, you must not desire me because you never want to be physically intimate." Surprised by his comment, she begins to list the times in recent weeks when she has made overtures that he has rebuffed. "Well, those weren't spontaneous efforts—they felt calculated," he declares. What is going on here? It seems as though no matter what action she takes, it is going to be a crash-and-burn experience. And that supposition would be fairly accurate.

Here is the pattern: When he was a child, he was rarely given physical attention by his parents. When they did hug him or reach out to him in some way, it always felt forced. They seemed to be much more comfortable with hugging his siblings. Hmm…it must be him, or so he assumed. As a result, he was starved for physical touch. He married young and thought his wife would now meet all those physical needs. While initially this seemed to be the case, she began to be less spontaneous with their intimacy. She did not hold his hand or touch him as frequently as she had in the past, but she was still just as physical as she had always been with their children. Boy, this felt familiar. Here he was, that rejected sibling all over again. Then, to put the nail in the coffin, it was discovered that she was having an affair.

A divorce takes place, some years go by, and he is remarried. All seems well at first, but then, as in most relationships, life gets busy, careers demand more time, and spontaneity is relegated to the back burner. This felt all too familiar. He knew exactly what was happening, or so he had convinced himself: his new wife was cheating on him and could not be trusted. But actually, this is not what was happening. His wife found him very attractive, as she stated, and absolutely loved their physical intimacy. As he made these proclamations that she no longer desired him, she was stunned. She attempted to initiate connection, only to be rejected. It didn't make any sense to her. He said he wanted closeness but then would sabotage any efforts that were made. He had put up walls with her. He no longer felt safe. But the truth of the matter is, it had nothing to do with her. He was playing out old patterns of issues in his past that had not been resolved. By not tackling those issues, he was dragging them into the present, and they were threatening to undermine his current marriage.

Intentionality #1—Commit yourself to clearing up the old junk that stands in the way of your relationship with your spouse. This is not easy, but it is necessary. If my desire is to regain (or honestly, it may be to gain for the first time) full closeness with my spouse, I need to work on my complete development as an individual. This may require implementing strategies that range from reading books to seeking therapy to staying present in those difficult times of communication with my spouse. Acquiring new communication tools can be an important part of that process as well. Much like turning the junk room in my house into a study, this process begins with me purposely and intentionally getting rid of the clutter.

Prepare Myself with Realistic Expectations

Earlier chapters examined the naïve picture of marriage that many couples initially had—a panacea for whatever ailed them. However, it quickly became clear from their disillusionment just how far off track people can get.

As the realization hit for many couples that all was not perfect, thoughts of throwing in the towel may have come quickly. "I didn't see this coming." "How could she think that?" "I can't believe he talked to me that way." And what quickly follows: "This marriage must be over."

For anyone who has been married for more than a few months, there is an awareness that unhappy times are inevitable. Wouldn't it have been much healthier if we had put that out there in the beginning?

I recently heard a speaker talk about taking his children fishing. He had been a pastor in Arkansas and was fortunate to have a Fish and Game official in his church. His friend would periodically call him to tell him where they had just stocked a lake. He might say, "We just put 1,000 trout into such-and-such a stream." Or, "We recently added 500 catfish to this pond." He would then take his kids to fish in those places. The children would cast their line it and pull out a fish. They would then cast it in again and pull out another. This was fun.

Once while the family was camping, the pastor discovered a nearby lake and asked his kids if they wanted to go fishing. They responded with excitement. As they settled in by the lake, his daughter cast in her line. After a minute, she pulled it out and cast it in again. Nothing. She then looked at her dad and said, "Something is wrong." Her dad replied that "sometimes you have to wait awhile for a fish." "This isn't fishing," she said. He responded, "Well, yes, this is fishing. What you have done before wasn't really fishing."

How much like marriage that is. We date, seeing each other regularly, and have a fun time. Then we get married, expecting that it will be the same level of pleasure without difficulties. Then we encounter problems we had never before considered, and we find ourselves thinking, "This is not marriage. This is not what a loving relationship is!" However, the reality is—yes, it is. What we experienced before was "the stocked stream."

We would be so much better prepared if we **acknowledged in the beginning of our marriage the inevitability of low points, times when relating will be difficult and things won't go as planned, but along with that, the assurance that we will get through them.** As Jeanette and Robert Lauer state so well, "In essence, a healthy approach would be to expect troubles, expect to work through those troubles, and expect the marriage to be stronger and more satisfying as a result."[4]

Intentionality #2—Embrace the knowledge that your marriage will have difficulties—it's guaranteed—but that you will pull together, you will have each other's back, and you will have the ability to grow in intimacy and unity.

When the Market Slumps, Invest

The stock market crash that took place in October 1929 had ramifications that would last for generations. In some instances, wealth evaporated overnight. Many families lost everything. The financial foundations of this country were rocked, and many legal safeguards were put in place as a result. Individuals like my father were labeled with a "post-Depression mentality." My dad would not throw anything away because he "might need it someday." He was frugal to a fault, and it was a by-product of the fear that was generated from the Depression.

While many lost their homes and their life savings, others made money. One such individual was J. Paul Getty. He took money that he received from an inheritance in 1930 and bought oil stocks that were massively depressed. One article states that "he snatched them up at bargain prices and created an oil conglomerate to rival Rockefeller."[5] He became a billionaire many times over. While the approach of many was to tightly hang on to what few dollars they had, others such as Getty saw an opportunity to invest when the market was down and create wealth—and that he did.

Not unlike individuals from the Depression era, many in troubled marriages today believe that they are best off cutting their losses and running. They have been hurt, and they are petrified at the thought of giving one more ounce of emotional energy to a marital relationship that has crashed. And yet, there is an opportunity for a different outcome. As author Scott Stanley states, "When your marriage is in a slump, it's the very best time to invest more. Investing in the relationship is the most powerful way to tell your mate that you're here and you're sticking."[6] In doing this, you are **taking the "big picture" approach.** And don't we desire the security that comes with knowing a spouse is here for the long haul?

Intentionality #3—When things are rocky and the love stocks have dipped in value, invest, invest, invest! When you take this approach, the return on your investment may surprise you. Of course there are exceptions to this, but most of us are not the exception. It probably won't be easy. You will have to **make some very intentional choices.** But I promise you, time and time again, I have seen it pay huge dividends.

Vulnerability

In order to stay above the radar and fly into the wild blue yonder, intentionality is required. And this is certainly true when it comes to a purposeful choice to be vulnerable. As some read this section, they will begin to feel as though I have just asked them to walk down Main Street naked with a loud speaker announcing their arrival. I think at some time in our lives, most of us have had weird nightmares like that. Believe me—I know it is frightening at worst and intimidating at best. But I want to offer a few suggestions to help you understand our innate longing for the safety of vulnerability as well as some of the behind-the-scenes entanglements that complicate being vulnerable.

The Perfect Easy Chair

I have discovered that after a long and stressful day at work, people like their chairs. Whether it is a chair they use for watching television, reading, or sleeping, they like their chairs. The days of a simple chair with four legs seem to be a thing of the past. People want their leather, vibrating, zero gravity recliners. One description reads:

> The zero gravity position cradles your back and elevates your legs above your heart, which is the position that doctors recommend as the healthiest way to sit. Easy ingress and egress are achieved with the extended range of motion in the upright position.... The brake control system is easy to use and extremely reliable. Wedge-shaped adjustable headrest cushion provides comfort for your head and neck...allows you to customize the optimum angle.[7]

You get the picture. And of course you can pick one of these chairs up for under $1500. As I said, people like their chairs.

Now at this point, you are probably wondering if I'm trying to pick up a few extra dollars marketing chairs. Well, not exactly. But there is an important visual here that I want you to see. I remember the opening of the 2000 film *The Patriot* starring Mel Gibson. The movie began with Gibson's character building a wooden rocking chair. As he finished his project, he gingerly eased into the chair, slowly putting his weight on it. When he thought it was safe to relax, the chair crumbled. In anger, he threw the pieces of the chair in a pile of his "previous chair" endeavors.

For me, these two images are pictures of marriage. Many of us have been wounded and hurt so many times we have lost count. We find ourselves approaching our mate much like the completed wooden rocking chair: we cautiously start to sit it in because it might not hold us, it might collapse—just as it has done dozens of times before. And when it does, we are once again disappointed. What we longed for when we married was the chair that we could confidently sit on, lean back in, prop our feet up with, and completely and fully sink and relax into. We all desire that kind of comfort and safety.

I appreciate Tim Keller's description of this when he writes, "When dating or living together, you have to prove your value daily by impressing and enticing. You have to show that the chemistry is there and the relationship is fun and fulfilling or it will be over. We are still basically in a consumer relationship, and that means constant promotion and marketing." He continues by stating, "The legal bond of marriage, however, creates a space of security where we can open up and reveal our true selves. We can be vulnerable, no longer having to keep up facades. We don't have to keep selling ourselves. We can lay the last layer of our defenses down and be completely naked, both physically and in every other way."[8]

Please don't misunderstand the image though. I am not saying that we get married and become uncaring slobs, no longer concerned with what our spouse thinks about us. Actually, as I comfortably and confidently relax fully into my marriage, I should find that I am even more motivated to be creative and loving toward my wife. I can do so knowing that even if I mess up a bit, there is a grace the wraps around me, from her, like that of a safe recliner. What I am saying is that we all desire to be able to fully and safely relax into our partnership. Knowing that is the desire for most people, I want to suggest that you find ways to **create that safe relational chair for your spouse.**

Begin with Assumed Positive Intent

Most all of us have been known to yell at our kids at one time or another. We may have overreacted to some misdeed and been unnecessarily harsh. If I were to observe you doing that and then say to you, "Wow, you really wanted to nail him to the wall and demean and crush his spirit," you would probably respond, "That was absolutely not my intent." Similarly, there are many times when we are in conflict with our spouse that we assume malicious intent from the get-go. We examined something similar in our earlier discussion regarding past hurts. A wife may appear grim so the husband assumes that she is angry with him. A husband may have noticed that his wife is withdrawn and assume that she feels no affection toward him. We are constantly observing our husband or wife's behavior and making interpretations about his or her intent—usually without any discussion. The problem with that is our interpretations may be completely wrong, and frequently are.

When you begin with an assumption that your spouse feels no affection toward you, for example, you will then react to her based upon everything going through that "feels no affection" lens. Based upon my beginning assumption, when she gets a cookie for herself without offering me one, it is another confirmation that she has no fondness toward me. My reactions to her will continue in that vein.

But what if...what if I assume positive intent? What if I assume that her being withdrawn is not about me? Perhaps it is about a situation with the kids, the neighbors, or a co-worker. I am going to begin with some type of assumption of intent. However, if I now am not interpreting her withdrawal as signifying a lack of fondness for me, I may not even notice that she didn't offer me a cookie. Or better yet, since I told her that I got on the scales yesterday and was disappointed that I had gained a few pounds and that I had better cut down on the sweets, now I might interpret her not offering me a cookie as her watching out for my welfare. Do you see how this takes the same events but processes them through a different lens? Viewing the scenario differently will, in turn, alter my responses to her.

Assuming positive as opposed to negative intent doesn't involve much risk. You have probably experienced your spouse leveling accusations against you regarding some of your intentions—and you knew they had missed the mark. So, in our quest to begin to enter vulnerability, I want to encourage you to **approach your spouse with an assumption of positive intent.**

Honest Pursuit

Several steps are required for an honest pursuit to begin. We will briefly examine the following: telling the truth, changing yourself first, celebrating differences, and maintaining a sense of humor.

Truth

As we begin to fly unafraid of detection, being truthful would seem like a no-brainer. And it's true that keeping our promises, honoring our agreements, not hiding secrets, and telling the truth are all part of that. But I want to focus particularly on being truthful about our feelings. You see, when we went underground and determined that it was no longer safe to be in our husband or wife's "line of sight," we also began hiding our feelings. Instead of expressing displeasure, we bit our tongue. Rather than show appreciation, which we feared would come back to haunt us, we kept our feelings to ourselves. When we longed for our spouse's support, it went unrequested, as we determined they wouldn't care. Allowing your mate to believe inaccurately that you feel a certain way about things is dishonest. As soon as he or she learns your true feelings, he or she will feel lied to, whether or not you even said anything. Learning to communicate with "I feel _____" messages can be the beginning of an emotionally honest relationship. If we think about it, dishonest emotions probably are the quickest way to destroy the bridges that connect us. The seeds of dishonest emotions are what typically lead to dishonest behaviors.

In the quest to reveal yourself honestly, **begin with truthful expressions of your feelings.**

Change Begins with You

One of the most powerful weapons against a "stuck" marriage is this principle: change begins with you. We have heard it hundreds of times, and we believe it: "If only our spouse would grasp the concept," we think. But believing it and putting it into action can be miles apart. Most "stuck" marriages that I see feature two individuals standing in opposite corners with their arms crossed, waiting for the other to change. As the years go by, resentments build and walls go up—but nothing changes. Even though we know that is the case, we are angry and we refuse to do it differently. But remember, you know what doesn't work—you've probably been doing that. You are reading this book because you want different results. I want you to have different results. Therefore, since you are the one reading, change begins with you.

In your journey to be transparent, **begin taking steps to change yourself first and to accept your partner unconditionally.**

Celebrate Differences

An almost magnetic force that draws us to our future mate is often our differences. Yet once we get married, for some bizarre reason we spend the next fifty years trying to make him or her be like us. How boring. If we are exactly alike, one of us is unnecessary.

We see things differently (no surprise there), and that is a good thing. As the Lauers explain, "Two people can look at the same thing, but focus on very different aspects. One person may look at a flower garden and find it hard to enjoy the flowers because he sees a few weeds. Another looks at the same garden, passes quickly over the weeds, and exults in the beauty of the flowers."9

Differences are differences. In other words, the fact that my wife loves shoe stores and I like Home Depot is different. One is not better than the other. Her shopping focus is not more right or wrong than mine. It is just different. While most of us would agree with that example, there are so many places where we get locked down in our minds in believing that those difference are bad things. What if instead of that mindset, we chose to go on an adventure—exploring our mate's "unknowability"?

Some of our differences are a result of old family scripts. They may be unique and helpful to us or they may require some purging. But really communicating with our mate about these differences can give us much greater insight and understanding of him or her. It is astonishing what can take place when we begin this simple endeavor: we really start to talk with each other, learning the best times to have certain conversations; we begin to discern subjects that are sensitive and areas where our spouse is fragile, recognizing our own brittleness in return; and we have the opportunity to make an amazing discovery—"I'm married to a very interesting person." And it only gets better. With the advancing of years and continued growth and development, you will have the opportunity to reacquaint yourself with your spouse time and time again. It will be anything but boring.

So, **celebrate your differences.** In doing this, we "rewire our brains, we rewrite old scripts, and so we change and grow in the deepest, most personal level of ourselves."10

Humor

It is difficult to watch couples that are more serious than a heart attack. You have probably encountered those whom you are convinced would come unraveled if they cracked a smile. I think of one wife who lives daily under what I would term the "tyranny of the serious." Living that way does not sound fun.

It is not at all surprising that studies confirm that happily married couples laugh together with greater frequency than unhappy couples.[11] Our most highly valued relationships are typically those that experience a high level of playfulness. As children we loved to laugh and play. Unfortunately for too many, they learned somewhere along the way that growing up meant you quit being silly. What a sad lesson. Playfulness enhances our communication and can be helpful in navigating sensitive topics. Humor can combat boredom, which is an insidious threat to marriages.

It is okay to embrace humor, so **laugh and play together.**

Soar

I want to summarize this chapter on ways to begin flying above the radar in your marriage, which will enable you to soar to new heights.

1. Be intentional in committing to clear out emotional junk around old hurts that hampers your relationship.

2. Embrace future challenges that are certain to come. Pull together and conquer them as a couple.

3. When the value of the relationship seems to dip, increase your emotional investment.

4. Create an emotional safe haven for your husband or wife.

5. Assume that your spouse intends well for you.

6. Be honest in your expression of emotions.

7. Make changes in yourself first.

8. Recognize your mate's unique qualities and celebrate your differences.

9. Laugh—be silly—play. Find humor wherever possible.

"A long marriage is two people trying to dance a duet and two solos at the same time."
—Anne Taylor Fleming[1]

Chapter Nine

Relearning the Dance

It had been a long time—a long time since they had ventured into these waters. Of course they could recall those early dating days when vulnerability had been so easy and so natural. It had not been difficult to be open and honest in their relationship. But then life had happened—all the disappointments in each other and feelings of emotional jeopardy, anger, withdrawal, and ultimately resignation. So now intentionality was intimidating work.

About a month and a half had passed since that afternoon conversation. With both joy and fear, they had agreed to try to carefully wade back into their relational pool. It was oh so easy to default into old patterns of relating that had never worked. While they knew those old patterns would never move them forward, they were still prone to repeat them because they were so good at them. Doug had "storming off and slamming doors" down to a fine art. Annie was a master at "complete withdrawal," and ran there all too quickly.

So, "intentionality" had become their new byword. If they were going to have any success at rebuilding, they would have to choose intentional actions over their go-to behaviors. Working to catch themselves before they defaulted each time had proven challenging. However, learning to extend more grace to each other had been helpful. This served as a nice invitation to vulnerability. However, if they thought intentionality was hard, staying exposed and vulnerable was nearly impossible at times. It didn't take much to cause them to run for cover.

One evening as Doug began to paint a word picture for Annie of his landscaping ideas for the backyard, she wrinkled her nose and sighed. "Ah, oh"—he had seen that response years before. That always meant that she thought it was a stupid idea and she couldn't believe that he would suggest such a lamebrain scheme (at least that is what he remembered). The mere wrinkle and sigh had stopped him in his tracks. Doug grew quiet and was about to leave the room. This threw Annie, but fortunately she didn't just accept the silence. Instead she said, "You quit telling me about the plan. Is something wrong?" He was about to say, "Nothing," when he realized that this is where vulnerability had to kick in. She had taken the risk of asking the question. Rather than run, he needed to stay in the moment and tell her what he was feeling.

So, he did. Of course, he had to think about it. Initially, he wasn't even aware of the reason for his discomfort. Exploring his feelings had not been something he was used to doing. As a matter of fact, he never thought she really cared much about what he thought or felt. So, he had kind of turned that switch off. But as he thought about it, he was able to honestly communicate to Annie the events of the past and how her sigh had triggered those same feelings of frustration and inadequacy that he had felt years ago. She listened and seemed to get it.

There was slow progress, which helped them to see possibilities. But it often seemed as though they were taking two steps forward and one and a half steps back. Glimmers of hope encouraged them; however, they were anxious to learn to make greater strides. They felt as though they needed to unlearn bad habits and relearn more effective strategies all at the same time. It reminded Doug of his first middle school dance—awkward, bumbling, and embarrassing, yet he had wanted to learn. Oh how he wanted to learn then—and he wanted to learn now.

Commitment to Friendship

This principle—that your spouse should be capable of becoming your best friend—is a game changer when you address the question of compatibility in a prospective spouse. If you think of marriage largely in terms of erotic love, then compatibility means sexual chemistry and appeal. If you think of marriage largely as a way to move into the kind of social status in life you desire, then compatibility means being part of the desired social class, and perhaps common taste and aspirations for lifestyle. The problem with these factors is that they are not durable. Physical attractiveness will wane, no matter how hard you work to delay its departure. And socio-economic status unfortunately can change almost overnight. When people think they have found compatibility based on these things, they often make the painful discovery that they have built their relationship on unstable ground.[2]

The statement above is far truer than most imagine. I am amazed day after day as I hear couples recount how they met and the narratives of their romance. They were attracted to each other, experienced the chemistry, connected in some manner physically, and their hormones were off to the races. And yet, here they sit—frequently feeling like strangers and not even liking one another. They don't view that person across from them as their friend, and here is the kicker—in many cases, they say they have never been friends. Now while that may seem counterintuitive, when the relationship develops in the manner suggested above, it really is not too surprising. They never took the time to become friends.

In one study that examined successful long-term marriages, researchers discovered that the first key to satisfaction is having a spouse that one truly considered to be his or her best friend and whom they honestly liked as a person.[3] This point cannot be overemphasized.

My wife and I knew each other in a work setting a couple of years before we ever began dating. During that time, we became friends. I recall once we were both in attendance at a workshop. At the end of the day, the presenters gave each participant two Jolly Rancher candies and asked us to give them to different people, telling them something we appreciated about them. Thinking this a fluffy, contrived exercise, I put mine in my pocket and took them back to my office. A couple of months later, my future wife was in my office, sharing with me that she had taken a job in a town about an hour away and would be commuting. She expressed her concern that all her friends would forget about her and she would lose those relationships. At this point, I took the Jolly Ranchers out of my desk drawer, handed them to her, and told her things that I had appreciated about her administrative abilities. But more importantly, I explained to her that these pieces of candy also represented a promise that I would still be her friend. To this day, I periodically give her a Jolly Rancher, reminding her that I am first and foremost her friend.

While many never develop friendships to begin with, others do but then later abandon that commitment. As a result, many marriages fall apart once the children leave home. You see, these parents may be quick to treat their relationship with the children "as a covenant relationship—performing the actions of love until their feelings strengthened—[while] they treated their marriages as a consumer relationship and withdrew their actions of love when they weren't having the feelings."[4] It should be no surprise, then, when relations with the kids remain strong and the marriage comes up empty, devoid of friendly thoughts and feelings.

I fully realize that if you are reading this book, there is a good chance that your spouse is not only not your best friend, but perhaps not any kind of friend. You find it difficult to even be in the same room with him or her and have a civil conversation. Please know that I understand. However, I want to suspend "what is" for a moment and ask you to imagine. Even if you have never truly been friends, I want you to imagine "what IF." We may have made a mess of this thing called marriage and settled into patterns that have created mistrust and dysfunction more damaging than we ever thought possible. You frequently hear, "You can't teach an old dog new tricks." While I understand the reasons for this statement, I totally disagree when it comes to people. I continue to do the things that I do professionally because I see rigid and stuck individuals soften and make radical change. What if radical change could happen in your relationships? Is it really possible to think that you could unlearn and relearn the bumbling dance steps you have been doing? I want to suggest you can. Let's look at learning how to truly, maybe for the first time, dance with our mate.

Dance

Much like Doug in the beginning of this chapter, I recall my first junior high after-school dance. While all the girls wanted to dance, and apparently had some idea how to, we guys were too cool to admit that we didn't even have a clue how to begin. Perhaps it was that experience that drove me to notice the coupon.

It was not that many years ago that I came across a coupon for a couple of sample dance lessons for twenty-five dollars. To this day, I am not sure what possessed me to redeem the offer. It was very intimidating. As I walked through the front door, I felt confident that the instructors would be able to take one look, discern that my dancing abilities were still at a junior high skill level, and politely ask me to leave. But instead, this young married couple, Krystal and Spencer, took my uncoordinated feet and made me into Fred

Astaire (just seeing if you are paying attention). Okay, perhaps they were good, but not that good. However, they did, over time, teach me some basic ballroom dance skills that actually enabled me to move around the dance floor with my wife in a not too dysfunctional and even somewhat coordinated manner.

While there were a number of techniques I learned, for our purposes here, there are six that I want to discuss: looking into your partner's eyes, leading and protecting, maintaining connection, negotiating closed and open positions, moving as one, and making your partner look good. So, leave the junior high gym and venture with me onto the marital dance floor.

Looking into Her Eyes

Showing up for my first dance lesson, I was nervous beyond belief. Surely, as Krystal led me onto the floor, she would see what a lost cause I was. I wanted to do well and was intent on not making mistakes. But it seemed that with each bit of instruction I would immediately make mistakes and amplify them. As I attempted the steps she taught me, I stared at the floor, willing my feet to take the correct movements in the appropriate direction. Repeatedly she brought my attention back to eye level and reminded me of the importance of looking into my partner's face.

This was an important concept for me to learn. It was easier for me when there were no other lessons going on and I didn't have to worry about running into anybody or anything, except the walls of course. But it brought home to me the principle of exclusivity. When I am on the dance floor with my wife, the only person that matters to me is her. She has my full, undivided attention. I am not looking around to gaze at other people's partners and wonder how their dancing is going; I am only looking at her.

If you want to experience success, it is essential that you adopt this position of exclusivity in your marriage. With this comes the element of restriction, which means some of your commitments must solely be given to your mate. I appreciate what Dr. Ronn Elmore says when he writes, "By definition *exclusivity* deliberately calls for the element of restriction in your intimate marriage relationship. It means some commitments therein are made available only to your covenant partner and to no one else. When covenant commitments are made available to anyone else, it is robbery of what you have already pledged to your mate alone."[5]

While most would nod their heads in agreement to this principle, I wonder how many of us have unknowingly (or perhaps knowingly) violated this agreement. In what ways have you possibly diverted your gaze from your dance partner's eyes? Perhaps it was a seemingly innocent flirtation with a co-worker. You think, "Well, that was just innocent play. He (or she) seems safe. No one meant anything by it." Perhaps, but as Jerry Jenkins so pertinently asks, "Then why does it bother us so much when we detect someone trying to flirt with our wives? A wink, a smile, a 'Hey, why don't you dump this guy and run off with me, ha ha,' a touch, and the hair on our necks bristles. Who does this guy think he is? He thinks this is funny?"[6] It bothers us because we want our mate to reserve those things for us.

I remember decades ago reading an interview with Patrick Duffy (who played Bobby Ewing on the television show *Dallas*) and his wife. The interviewer asked his wife if Patrick's love scenes with his on-screen wife, Victoria Principal, ever bothered her. She said that most of the time she was okay, as she knew he was just acting. However, occasionally she would observe a scene in which he would do some little thing with Victoria's hair or give his co-star some special wink, and she found herself feeling as though something had just been diminished. She had believed that special look was reserved for her alone, and here she was seeing her husband give it away on screen to someone else. She felt robbed.

Flirting is fun. I do it all the time—with my wife. Whether we play footsie under the table at a family dinner, I wink at her across a crowded room, or I send her seductive texts when she is in the middle of a school board meeting, I flirt with her. It can give us a rush and is pleasurable. And with my wife, it is safe. I give her what belongs only to her and no one else.

There are many ways that we can take our eyes off our husband or wife: "Facebooking" an old high school/college boyfriend or girlfriend, talking about problems in our marriage to an opposite-sex "friend" at work, even inappropriate inside jokes with the opposite sex. One good test is to ask ourselves the question, "If I saw my spouse behaving in this manner, how would I feel?" If I would feel betrayed, cheated, or as though something had been taken from the private specialness of our relationship, that should be a red flag.

On the dance floor or in my marriage, my eyes are exclusively on my partner—period!

Leading and Protecting

Prior to the 1960s, the majority of Americans accepted the premise that the husband was the "head" or "leader" of the household. However, through the changing social climate of the sixties and seventies, that role began to be seriously called into question. While there are many reasons for that shift, no doubt, one is the fact that men so grossly abused that position. Husbands were selfish, demanding, and domineering. It didn't take too many decades of that before women began to say, "I've had enough," and understandably so.

With that evolved some very confusing marital roles. Needless power struggles emerged with no clear leadership guidelines and agreements. I have actually had couples in my office who were so immersed in this type of struggle that I have sent them to see Krystal for a few dance lessons. I wanted to get them onto the dance floor so that they could physically see what happens if their conflict were to continue. Most often, in ballroom dancing, the woman takes steps backwards to the man's forward lead. Since she cannot see where he is leading them, it is the responsibility of the man to protect and direct their steps.

In the Book of Ephesians 5:22-33, God gives us some pretty clear leadership guidelines. I would encourage you to read that passage in order to get the full flavor of it, but I want to summarize those verses in a couple of statements. First, the writer says that women are to submit to their husband's leadership (see Eph. 5:22). Now I know that may cause the hair on the back of many women's necks to bristle because of the ways in which this has been abused. But, secondly, the next paragraph in that passage truly defines what that leadership for men is to look like. You see, we as men are to lead in our marriage with a sacrificial love to be willing to lay down our very lives for our wives and to commit to helping keep them radiant and without stain or blemish. This loving relationship between a husband and wife is designed to be a reflection of God's love with His people. God leads His people in a loving, protective dance, and we husbands are to do the same with our wives. I want to suggest that in our marriages, there are two important factors to this leading and protecting—guarding our boundaries and establishing security.

Leading with Guarded Boundaries

While on the dance floor, the man is usually in the leading role. Yet there are occasions, depending on the movement, when the man could be the one taking the backward steps. I mention that because it is important for both me and my wife to guard our boundaries, whether on the dance floor or in our marriage.

It is so very easy to drop our guard and not protect those boundaries. I frequently hear individuals make statements like, "I need more from him" or, "She is not meeting my needs." And when they begin to feel these ways, if they are not intentionally keeping their boundaries intact, danger can creep in. Those outside of your marriage rarely have as much at stake as you do. As a result, they will gladly plow down your boundaries and run roughshod over your vows. This is commonly seen, as the following letter reflects:

I helped lead a Bible study for women facing marital struggles. I saw these women through pain in their marriages and even separations. But I was different. I was faithful and true. When we finally purchased a computer, I found that the Internet contained so many interesting places. I could look up vacation spots, read newspapers. These were all good things, nothing evil. I never realized that I was only a click away from destruction.

> One day I signed up for a chat room. I chose a clean one, not a porn room. I wanted to just go in and see what was going on. Almost immediately a man began talking to me. He paid attention to me and had insightful responses to every word I wrote.
>
> I continued to meet this man in the chat room, even though I knew it was wrong. The relationship seemed innocent. We just talked about family and life. Soon we progressed to phone calls. I loved communicating with him. He cared so much.
>
> After some time, we decided to meet. We were in love, or so we thought. After telling my husband I was meeting some girlfriends, I took off and hooked up with this man for what I thought would be a romantic weekend getaway. It wasn't at all what I expected, and suddenly everything came crashing down. I had betrayed my husband and my family.
>
> My careless involvement with the Internet nearly destroyed my marriage. I became addicted, and it eventually led to an affair. I have regretted the day when, with one click on the mouse, I entered a downward spiral of sin and deception. I failed to build a fence of protection around my marriage. I didn't guard my heart.[7]

Rarely do individuals set out to plan the moral disaster such as the one described above. But it is critical that we plan NOT to. About fifteen years ago, I was driving a friend's truck, pulling a horse trailer full of fencing materials. It was a heavy load, but it seemed to handle well. However, when the driver in front of me slammed on her brakes, I couldn't avoid hitting her. You see, I needed greater braking power, and I certainly needed to allow more stopping time.

Author Robert Abbott says, we "must learn to keep plenty of space between us and sinful acts, so we can start braking soon enough to stop before it is too late."[8] He offers a list of situations that may require us to heighten our braking awareness. Here are just a few that I feel are critical to the safety of our marriages and that I have adapted from that list: when you are so busy there is no time to be alone with God; when you are too busy to spend at least one relaxed evening a week with your spouse and family; when you feel you deserve more attention than you are getting at home; when you wouldn't want your husband/wife or colleagues to see what you're reading or looking at; when the romance in your marriage is fading; when your charisma, appearance, and personality are more attractive to the opposite sex and you are tempted to make the most of it; when you enjoy fantasizing about an illicit relationship; when a person of the opposite gender makes himself or herself available by his or her behavior; when someone other than your mate tells you how wonderful you are and how much he or she loves you; when you think Scriptures concerning adultery are for others, not you; when you start feeling sorry for yourself; and when you hope God isn't looking or listening.[9]

Another area in which boundary guarding is important is the realm of physical touch. I appreciate the protective stance that author Jerry Jenkins takes for his marriage when he says that in greeting a woman, he might shake hands or squeeze an arm or a shoulder. However, he only embraces dear friends or relatives—and only then in front of others.[10] Now to some, this may seem a bit overprotective, but his description of what often transpires when people relax this boundary, engaging in greater physical touch, is all too accurate:

> For instance, what would happen if I just lingered an instant to see what kind of reaction I might get? And let's say that reaction was encouraging. We might both pretend it didn't happen, but what about the next time? Would we not be carefully checking each other out to see if what we thought we felt the first time was accurate? And what if it was? At what point would we overtly embrace passionately, silently declaring our feelings for each other?
>
> I don't know, and I don't want to know. That's why I keep such activity public, ensuring its appropriateness.[11]

From both professional and personal experiences, I want to applaud this stance and state clearly that he is spot-on.

Protecting with Fortified Security

I have been captivated by the histories of castles in Europe. Many of these castles in countries such as England, France, Italy, and Spain originated in the ninth and tenth centuries. There were tens of thousands of these fortified residences that were built, most often, for defensive purposes. I am amazed at the innovation that went into the various designs and the elaborate expense incurred for protection. Over time, towers and moats were added for protection. A typical wall ranged from ten feet to thirteen feet thick and was known to extend at times to over fifty feet in height.[12] Needless to say, these people were serious about their security.

While each of the various features of the castle served a significant purpose, it is interesting to note that castle builders recognized the entrance as the weakest part of the defense. Because of this, they developed components such as the gatehouse to control the flow of traffic. There were also openings in the ceiling of the gatehouse that allowed for the pouring of boiling oil and molten lead on their attackers. **Staying more diligent at the gatehouse of our marriages would help us restrict who and what we let in that could harm our union.** I am confident that if we approached our marriages with the same determination for safety, many problems would be averted.

While writing the previous paragraph, I received a call from a client describing an explosion between him and his wife yesterday. It reminded me of a key component for security, and that is vulnerability. Initially, you may think those two opposite concepts. But while we need secure defenses for the outside of our castle, we must be vulnerable to those on the inside with whom we are serving as fellow warriors—or in the case of our marriages, our spouse. As my client experienced, exhibiting resistance to being open and vulnerable with his spouse (his fellow warrier) creates feelings of insecurity in her relationship with him. We are hesitant to open up because this makes us vulnerable and that creates risk. We may be uncertain how our mate will respond to our vulnerability, and therefore we avoid the risk. However, I contend that, like those battling together in the castle, until we work through our fear of risk with our spouse, we will not have security.

Have you ever seen a couple who appeared to have it all together only to hear later on that they have divorced? How could this be? I would suggest that they have taken care of neither their outside walls nor their inside connections of vulnerability. Those who develop these pieces of security in their relationship have been compared by author Gary Smalley to a bamboo tree. I love the picture that he paints and want to share it here:

> The Chinese bamboo tree may look like it's not developing as it should, but remarkable things are happening underground. The tree is busy putting out thick and long-ranging roots called rhizomes. The plant limits its

surface growth while its network of roots reaches deep and wide, providing a firm base for massive growth. If you looked at a young Chinese bamboo tree in its fourth year, you might think, *that is the puniest, most pathetic tree I've ever seen. It's been sitting there several years without any noticeable growth. There must be something wrong with it.* So you decide to pull it up. You take hold of that tiny tree and pull with all your might. Nothing happens. So you yank, and jerk, and twist, and tug, but the tree doesn't budge. No matter how much sweat and energy you put into it, you cannot pull that Chinese bamboo tree out of the ground.

Then in the fifth year of growth, the Chinese bamboo tree shoots up to a staggering height of eighty feet. Can you imagine? Something that had been growing without much visible progress for four years in the next year alone develops into an eighty-foot tree![13]

If we are to avoid crashing and burning on the marital dance floor, it is imperative that we learn the concepts of leading and protecting in our relationship. Protecting our boundaries with and for our spouse and creating rhizome-like security are essential.

Maintaining Connection

If a couple desires to move around the ballroom dance floor in an elegant fashion, making and maintaining a connection is a must. This begins with the man's frame in preparation to ask the woman to dance and in turn her acceptance of his invitation. The sequence looks something like this: the gentleman extends his left hand, beckoning the woman to the dance; she steps forward, accepting his hand with her right hand; she faces him, slightly off-center to his right; he places his right hand on her back, just beneath her shoulder blade; and she places her left hand on his upper arm. There are some other specifics as to the turning and positioning of their heads, which helps them maintain balance. Keeping these points of connection enables her to sense his lead and truly allows them to move in a cohesive flow. Invariably, the most common difficulty that my wife and I experience on the dance floor is either my ineffective leading—because she can only follow my clear directions—or the loss of our connection. When our connection isn't maintained, she cannot accurately sense my lead and it leaves her guessing, which is almost always a ballroom disaster. If I am leading well (or so I think) but we are not connected, the result is the same as if I am not leading at all.

One of the most interesting aspects of the connection between dance partners is that there is tension in the connection. For example, as I am holding my wife's right hand with my left one, there is a push-pull feel. By her hand slightly pulling against my pull or pushing against my push, sensitivity to the leading is encouraged and a better connection is made. This enables us to move in even tighter sync with one another.

This same push-pull connection is recorded in the creation account in Genesis 2:18. An intriguing combination of words is used here when the Scriptures state that *"the Lord God said, 'It is not good for the man to be alone. I will make him a helper suitable for him'"* (Genesis 2:18). The word in Hebrew that is translated "suitable" actually conveys some of the following ideas: "over against," "corresponding to," "counterpart," and "in opposition to."[14]

I believe that when most of us read this passage and see "suitable helper," we think that the relationship with our spouse should be a smooth, agreeable, no-conflict partnership. But this is not what God intended at all. His purpose wasn't always agreement, but it was to create a life of beauty. He desires for us to move across the dance floor of life as one—dancing with a fluidity that screams "known/loved partners." But as we saw in ballroom dance, that grace of movement can only happen when there is tension in the connection, when the push-pull dynamic creates a sensitive leading and following that allows us to complement and correspond to each other. We are like two different puzzle pieces that fit together to form a complete picture.

One feature on the dance floor that can be unnerving is other people. They are unpredictable, causing us to have to modify the steps we had planned. Similarly, life throws us curves and changes that we had not anticipated. As a matter of fact, during the course of your marriage, you and your spouse will both grow and change—guaranteed. For some, this is traumatic. For others, it is new and exciting. I promise you, the person with whom you will grow old will be a very different person from the one you married—and you will be every bit as different for them. Maintaining a solid connection throughout your marital dance will enable you to navigate those changes much more smoothly.

Negotiating Open and Closed Positions

In the previous section, we discussed the various connecting points that are so very critical to sensing and responding to movement on the dance floor. But just when I thought I was beginning to feel relatively secure and could take a breath of relief, my dance teacher taught me about open and closed positions. With the appropriate connecting, we had been in "closed position." It felt safe and protected. But now she wanted me to let go, break connection, and move somewhat independently of my partner. My anxiety increased as I worried about all the things that were sure to go wrong.

There are two levels of "open position" on the dance floor. One example would be when my partner does a 360-degree turn in front of me. We remain in hand contact during the turn and then she returns to our connected frames, or our closed position. In other, more complicated steps, we break connection completely and she steps away to do her own steps, as I do likewise, and then she returns to me. Sometimes, depending on the steps of the dance, I may need to step aside and create room for her as she returns to where I once stood. But by doing so, we are able to reconnect and continue our dance.

Whether on the dance floor or in life, most of us actually gravitate to the open position. Think about it for a minute: if you attend a typical dance, most couples are standing in some proximity with each other, but they generally are doing their own thing. The music ends, they stop their gyrations, and they walk their partner back to sit down. This is far easier and involves less risk than actually engaging with your partner on the dance floor, learning to move in a coordinated fashion.

Unfortunately, people in the dance of life have often been wounded—deeply. If I were to liken it to ballroom dance, their feet haven't just been stepped on; they have been stomped on, leaving them with broken toes. As a result, getting close, in a closed-position relationship, is more than scary. They may have been censored, laughed at, or physically abused by their parents or in their previous opposite-gender relationships. For them, closeness has not been safe.

It is sad to me to find individuals who desire to have someone close but who, because of their negative experiences, will substitute drama for closeness. Think about individuals you know who seem to constantly be in the middle of some kind of drama: "She did this to me." "He said this about her." "How dare they say that!" "Who do they think they are?" "Can you believe that waiter got my order wrong?" The proverbial pot always seems to be stirred, and we scratch our heads in bewilderment. I contend that for many, drama gives the illusion of engagement and closeness when it is actually the exact opposite. By maintaining the illusion, we think we have less at risk. However, the truth of the matter is that if I just stand over in the corner of the room and move to the music by myself, I may look as though I am dancing, but I honestly am missing it. If I avoid risk by choosing drama, I truly risk losing any genuine intimacy.

Occasionally in the midst of the drama is a co-dependent relationship. If while in a 360-degree turn on the dance floor, my wife stumbled and fell, I would quickly rush to her aid, which she would appreciate. However, if every time I released her to move into an open position, she fell just so I would run and embrace her, this would be a very strange dance. Yet many engage in this manner of relating. As a couple seems to be approaching some level of healthy independence, a partner who feels unsafe with this may engage in unhealthy behaviors for the purpose of keeping the other dependent. This can be accomplished by items such as alcoholism, eating disorders, and even mental and physical health issues.

My relationship with my spouse is designed to be a healthy cycle of dependence and independence. We value the ability to make our own decisions about matters and come together on others. Our respective careers are different from one another and yet important to and supported by each other. On a weekday afternoon, we may be dancing in open position, but we know that later in the day we will be back in closed-position contact with each other—connecting, sensing, and reaffirming our dance together. It is because of the safe, coordinated movement together that we each feel secure dancing during the day in open position. We confidently know that at the end of the independent steps, our partner will be standing right where we expect him or her to be, taking us back into his or her arms.

Moving as One

We have looked at some of the keys to creating a beautiful dance on the ballroom floor: looking exclusively into our partner's eyes; learning to lead, protect, and follow with guarded boundaries and security in the relationship; maintaining connections that truly allow us to be partners; and learning the art of open and closed positions, which provide required levels of dependence and independence. When we are able to do these things consistently on the dance floor and in our marriage, we begin to move as one in a harmonious life. Please don't misunderstand—I didn't say the dance is perfect and we are syrupy sweet and happy all the time. I said we "begin" to move, and life does indeed "become" more united. I still make missteps and blow turns and even step on feet, but I am getting better.

While I could address many areas that are involved in helping us move through life with our partner as "one," I want to look just briefly at two.

First is the area of sexual intimacy. This is a topic that is at the forefront of our culture's mind and strangely absent from most couple's conversations. Yet it is one of the most critical components of a great marriage. I want to adapt just a few suggestions made by Mark O'Connell in *The Marriage Benefit*:

1) We must make a concerted effort to become real about our bodies. Here is an astounding fact: our bodies will age. Maybe that is not so astounding, but our culture's airbrush mindset drives us to the point that people chase after an ageless body. However, it doesn't exist. As O'Connell instructs, "Work on the emotional side of your relationship; our perceptions of attractiveness are mediated by our feelings for each other. The better we feel about each other the better we look to each other."[15]

2) We have to stop dismissing the "it doesn't mean anything" ideas about pornography and seductive dress. Visuals stimulate—especially men. And women have been cast in the roles of "sexual playthings" for long enough. It is important that we not just avoid this issue but that we actively oppose it.

3) Don't worry so much about trying to have "great" sex. "Instead risk being real with each other. Believe in sex that stumbles, that laughs, that makes a point of being human."[16]

4) If sexual intimacy is missing from your relationship, acknowledge the problem and be willing to talk about it. It is always amazing to me that sex is one of the most intense focuses of energy in a new

relationship, yet it is one of the least discussed areas in a marriage. I recognize that people have insecurities about how they look and how they perform. Yet I want to say clearly, if people don't communicate about their sexual relationship, it will not get better! We must normalize sex. We talk about other areas in our marriage when they don't work best, and this area must be no exception. While we may feel shame or embarrassment or uncertainty, as we begin to move in the dance as one, we must risk entering into a discussion about this most sensitive and important area. It can only improve the dance.

5) Laugh, smirk, giggle. Don't take sex too seriously. I almost want to encourage people to have lousy sex sometimes, just so that it doesn't get too intense. We have been raised in a culture where we think that sex is supposed to be what we see on the movie screen—two people running across the screen toward each other in slow motion, meeting in a lip-locked embrace that culminates in simultaneous orgasms. If we experience anything less, it is subpar and indicative of catastrophic problems. Not so. It means we are humans with complicated sexualities. Lighten up when things go wrong. Laugh when you inadvertently fall off the bed. These are the things that make our relationship interesting.[17]

Our sexual relationship is to be enjoyed in the context of our dance—when it goes smoothly as well as when we blunder. Relax, be playful, and most importantly, talk about it all—fears, desires, and needs, as well as how much you enjoy sharing the experience with your mate.

The second area vital to moving smoothly as one is the area of spiritual intimacy. Jeremiah 29:11 says, *"For I know the plans I have for you,' says the Lord. 'They are plans for good and not for disaster, to give you a future and a hope'"* (NLT). This is a declaration for you and your marriage today. It is a proclamation of God's purposes, and it is spiritual intimacy that links you to these purposes.

I appreciate the Rosbergs' simple definition of this principle. While many may believe there is something weird or mystical about this, they state otherwise: "Spiritual intimacy occurs when you as husband and wife surrender your lives and relationship to the Lord. You bond and grow together spiritually when you live out your marriage relationship according to God's ways and aim to please Him in all things."[18]

We usually connect initially with our future spouse due to some physical attraction. This may then develop into something even stronger as a result of emotional attachments. But over the long haul it is our spiritual intimacy that solidifies our relationship. It provides opportunities for the deepest levels of communication and "permits profound sharing you cannot enjoy at any other level."[19]

Make Each Other Look Good

Now if I were strictly writing about dance, my last piece of advice would be to make her look good, because one of the man's goals on the ballroom dance floor is to make his woman look good. Even though he may feel as though he is doing the hardest work by leading and protecting, he is not to be the object of notice; his partner is. By leading effectively, the male sets the stage for the female to dance well. It is her movements that give grace and elegance to the dance.

As the leader in my marriage, I am to have the same goal. Like we read in Ephesians 5 earlier, my highest calling in my marriage is to present my wife as radiant, white as snow, without wrinkle or blemish—in other words, make her look good (see Eph. 5:25-27). Yet I would submit that when we dance or live life in a manner that operates based on the principles of exclusivity, security, connectivity, interdependence, and unity in movement, we both look good.

Relearning

I am happy to tell you that my dance teacher was able to make progress with this inept junior high school dancer. By acquiring the new skills discussed above, I was able to unlearn bad habits and relearn how to dance. I don't come close to having it down yet—either on the dance floor or in my marriage. But I am better. I move more effectively in both arenas, making fewer mistakes, and we even look more like an actual dancing couple. And I promise you, if I can relearn the relational dance, you can too. I may not have a twenty-five-dollar coupon for you, but here is what I do have—begin to integrate the steps above into your relationship, and I guarantee you that the dance will begin to change.

"Don't ever stop dating your wife and don't ever stop flirting with your husband."
—Unknown[1]

Chapter Ten

Where Your Treasure Is...

While it had been raining off and on all week, this morning it was sunny and the skies were clear. Doug had been looking forward to this Saturday for several weeks, as he had a tee time scheduled with three of his good friends.

Normally Doug tried to play golf at least a couple of times a month, but lately, unusual demands at work had caused him to put in some extra Saturdays, which had taken a toll on his ability to get out and play. So, this morning he found himself feeling almost giddy.

Annie had woken up early and made a quick run to the grocery store to pick up a few things for a barbeque they were hosting that evening. She was looking forward to this event, as it would be the first time she and Doug had done any entertaining in "longer than she could remember."

They were feeling like they were in a pretty good place. After being so near the brink of throwing in the towel and calling it quits on their marriage, they were making significant improvements. With bridges of trust being rebuilt, they were both finding it a bit easier to be more transparent and vulnerable with the other. The more they learned to partner up and safely connect, the less alone each felt. Besides that, they were actually having fun doing stuff together and were enjoying hanging out. They had all but given up hope that this would ever be happening again, but here they were.

Annie marveled at the initiative Doug had been taking recently to do special things for her. For example, he came home the previous week and told her, "Happy birthday" (her birthday was still five months away) and gave her a present—ten lessons for the two of them at the nearby ballroom dance studio. She was blown away. Over the years she had hinted to Doug of her interest in this, but he had never responded. Yes, things were moving in a new direction that was exciting and life-giving.

As Annie arrived home from the store, she found Doug pacing. She had inadvertently taken the car that Doug kept his golf clubs in, and he was anxious to leave. However, first he went out to help her bring things in. As he opened the trunk and found the groceries piled on top of his golf clubs, he hit the ceiling. He could not believe that Annie would just pile potatoes, canned goods, and boxes on top of his prized possession. Walking back into the house, he slammed a cereal box down, demanding to know what she was thinking. Didn't she know how much he had spent on those clubs and how meticulously he took care of them? How could she be so careless? For five minutes he berated her, hardly stopping to breathe. Finally, he said, "I just can't believe that what is so important to me means so little to you."

Wisely, Annie paused, then simply responded with, "You are correct, I was careless. I'm sorry. I hope you can forgive me." This response took the wind out of Doug's tirade. Then Annie said, "Please know that what is important to you is important to me. I only wish that I were as important to you as those golf clubs are. I hope that someday you will want to painstakingly care for me as you do those clubs."

Doug was speechless. He immediately realized that his response to her had been ridiculous and over the top. Yet it was too late to take it back, and he knew that any words he might offer right now would probably feel obligatory and weak. But more significant than all of that was the sting of her words. He knew they were accurate, and he hated that. Of course he loved Annie, but she was correct—he demonstrated greater care for those sticks of graphite than he did his wife and partner. He felt about two inches tall. He knew that he still had some "priority issues" to deal with. What had he heard the pastor say last week about his treasure and his heart?

Treasuring

"When I walk on the beach to watch the sunset, I do not call out, 'A little more orange over to the right, please,' or, 'Would you mind giving us less purple in the back?' No, I enjoy the always-different sunsets as they are. We do well to do the same with people we love."[2] This quote by psychologist Carl Rogers is a fitting description for treasuring.

In Matthew 6:21, Jesus makes the statement, *"For where your treasure is, there your heart will be also."* But what exactly does this mean?

As a child, when I thought of treasure, visions of gold coins and strands of jewels all heaped in a giant chest came to mind. If you have ever seen the movie *Pirates of the Caribbean,* or have been on the ride by the same name in Disneyland, you may have similar images when thoughts of treasure capture your imagination. In both the ride and the movie, it is clear that the desire (actually, the all-consuming pursuit) is for the pirates to get their hands on the untold riches. It drives them to all forms of greedy and deceitful choices.

One of my favorite movie trilogies is The Lord of the Rings series. In these movies, there is a ring that embodies tremendous power, and many are intent on getting it. One character named Gollum (or Sméagol) is driven, seemingly by every fiber of his existence, to acquire this ring. He will steal it, kill for it—he will do whatever it takes to possess it.

Now while I certainly don't advocate greed, murder, and deceit, I believe that these two movie images depict clearly this concept that Jesus presents. Where my treasure is—in other words, what I value most—will capture my heart. If I put money in a new stock, I may constantly check *The Wall Street Journal* to see how my investment is doing. If I buy a classic sports car, my free time might be spent washing, waxing, and babying it. If I treasure my spouse—truly treasure him or her—it will alter how I live my life at a relational level. I wonder how many of us pursue our spouses with the same passion as Captain Jack Sparrow chasing after his pirate's gold, or Gollum in his relentless, single-minded focus of possessing the ring. I am convinced that if we were this diligent in a passionate pursuit of our husband or wife, the divorce rate in this country would plummet.

Notice that Jesus doesn't say, "The things that make your heart go pitter-patter will become the things that you treasure." It is the exact opposite. As I regularly advise couples, the choices and decisions upon which you act will put in motion the feelings you will experience. We feel what we feel because of what we believe. The things to which I commit time, effort, and focus are those which will capture my heart. I always find it interesting that while spouses seem uncertain of how to treasure each other, like Doug in the beginning of this chapter, they are crystal-clear on how to treasure their golf clubs, boats, diamond earrings, Louis Vuitton purses, and any number of other items.

Treasuring, honoring, making a priority, imparting value to—these are all descriptions of what you and your spouse both desire in relation to one another. In looking back to Carl Rogers's quote at the beginning of this section, we want to be admired and appreciated by our spouse for who we are, as we are—just like that sunset observed while walking along the beach. Gary Smalley reports that honor is such a vital principle in marriage that researcher Dr. John

Gottman can predict divorce just by observing whether spouses honor each other.[3]

There are many ways to honor and treasure our mates. One wife recently reported to me that for her birthday, her husband gave her a seemingly token gift that deflated her—that is, until she opened the card and found the keys to a new car. While that is exciting and certainly feels honoring, most couples say that it does not take over-the-top actions such as this to make one feel valued. Instead, it requires consistent small things. Dr. Ronn Elmore states that "modest but frequent gestures of affection and care may individually appear slight and inconsequential, but grouped together over days and years they become the undeniable evidence of your highest love and deepest devotion."[4] I would adapt this and add that your diligence in the small things becomes undeniable evidence of the treasuring of your spouse.

Even though we appreciate being honored, we also easily get caught up in the busyness of life and default to what we consider to be basic honoring behaviors. For men it might be focusing on working and providing for the family. Many men assume that their wives know how they feel and therefore forget to communicate it. Likewise women get focused on the things clamoring for their attention such as their jobs, the kids, or household responsibilities. And with their attention being consumed, they may lose sight of demonstrating honor to their husbands.

If it is true that what I treasure will determine the condition of my heart—and I believe it is—and if it is equally important that my spouse occupies first place in that position of honor in order for my marriage to begin to flirt with healthiness, where do I start? How can I best begin this journey of honoring and treasuring my spouse? I want to look at eight different steps we can take to begin to 1) communicate importance and value to our spouse and 2) develop changed hearts.

1. ***Own Your Own Stuff***

When it comes to "your stuff" (boats, cars, toys), you may not want anybody to mess with it because it is yours and you absolutely own it. But when it comes to your emotional stuff, you probably try to get as far away from that as you can. We tend to be pretty selfish in this area. If I am angry, it is because somebody else made me that way. When I am frustrated, it is surely due to another person's inappropriate behaviors. We are a selfish bunch. I want my material things, but I want you or someone else to be responsible for how I feel.

As I observe couples in conflict, I am often mildly entertained as I watch their mental gymnastics at work. It really isn't so much that husbands and wives doesn't realize when they are in the wrong—because subconsciously, they know when their behaviors need to be corrected. But they take the selfish road by trying to get their spouses to change their behaviors so that they won't have to go through the painful process of self-examination and make necessary corrections. While we may be able to push the blame onto our spouse for a period of time, eventually it will lead to a rift in our relationship.

Think about times when your mate has tried to blame you for what you knew was their "stuff." My guess is that you felt disrespected, degraded, and discounted. What you did not feel was honored or treasured. Before I make any other efforts at honoring my spouse, I must take care of this issue first. A willingness to be responsible for my own emotions and behaviors is the foundation for all other honoring efforts. Without this first step, any others will fall short.

2. ***Outdo Each Other***

I am not talking about a competition, but rather an attitude. I hear couples talk about the need for a marriage to be fifty-fifty.

While that may seem reasonable at first glance, the reality is that it leads to what I would call a "ledger book" relationship. In other words, we constantly keep a tally going in our heads as to what we have each contributed to the relationship. "I unloaded the dishwasher the last two times so it is only fair that you do so the next two." This kind of accounting becomes wearisome, and it will lead to partners feeling devalued. Instead, I urge you to approach each other with an attitude of, "How can I serve him or her today?" Instead of keeping track of who does what, how about you view what needs to be done as an opportunity to serve your spouse?

Now I recognize that if you are not both on the same page about serving each other, you can feel taken advantage of. Some will tell me, "If I worked to out-serve her, she would never do anything and I would wind up doing it all." I am not suggesting that you do it all and find yourself in a relationship of indentured servitude. I am merely encouraging a change of attitude in how you work to honor one another.

We live in a culture that is all about "me." In adopting that social philosophy, we lose the sense of "we." We fear that somehow, if we focus on the "we," we will lose ourselves. Yet I would contend that the exact opposite is true. Mark O'Connell phrases this so appropriately when he says, "We are not beings unto ourselves, rather we are who we are by way of our relationships. This principle is captured by a wonderful South African word—ubuntu. Loosely translated, ubuntu means "I am because we are."[5] What a beautiful picture—and it is achieved when I am committed to serving my spouse full on.

3. Give Your Time

Treasuring sounds like such a noble and worthy concept. But if we don't actually demonstrate it in action, it becomes a lonely and hollow word. This is found to be especially true when it comes to time. Dr. Gary Chapman even lists quality time as one of the five basic love languages. Spending time with someone is one of the most convincing ways of saying, "You are important."

The hectic pace at which we live our lives seems absolutely crazy sometimes. And I completely get it because I do it as well. We find ourselves talking to certain people on our cell phones only when we are driving. We text because we don't have time to talk. Pausing to sit down on a corded phone attached to the wall (some may not even remember those days) and talking for an extended period of time seems a distant memory. But truly, if you want to give someone a gift of honor, give that person your time. My time is one of my most precious resources, and there is no better place for me to spend it than on my most precious possession—my marriage. When I do so, my wife knows that she is important to me.

4. *Sacrifice and Serve*

These are words that perhaps come to mind when we think of members of the military who have given their lives in defense of our freedoms. However, when it comes to our relationships, we often are more interested in whether or not the relationship is meeting our needs: Is the other person serving me?

In a study conducted regarding sacrifice and service, researchers discovered that the more committed individuals were to their relationship, the more willing they were to give up activities that they considered to be important to them for the benefit of the relationship.[6] While that particular finding may not be too surprising, they also found that people who were most inclined to sacrifice for their mate were also the happiest in their relationships and, as one might expect, were most likely to continue in them.

When we are willing to relinquish our rights to important activities for the sake of our marriage, we declare to our husband or wife, "You are more important to me than those things. You are cherished."

5. *Touch*

Touch is one of the most neglected areas in honoring our most important earthly relationship. Now as I say that, some of you may be thinking either, "Oh great, he is going to tell me that I have to give my spouse more sex" or, "Great, he is going to tell my spouse that he or she needs to give me more sex!" But I am not talking about sex here. I work with far too many couples who engage in regular sexual intimacy and yet feel physically neglected. I repeatedly hear from wives who say, "I always know when he wants sex—he holds my hand or gives me a hug. It is the only time he touches me." And they resent it. Yes, sexual connection is an important part of our marriage, but when couples attempt to meet all their needs for touch through sexual contact only, they are left feeling used and disconnected.

If you have ever had a massage, you know how relaxing and life-giving that can be. I read about one massage therapist who massaged her young son nearly every day of his life and, as a result, he had never been sick. Now while I am not suggesting that massage is a panacea for all of life's ills, I am saying that non-sexual, sensitive, caring touch has health benefits. We were designed for touch. When your spouse caresses your shoulder, touches your arm as she walks through the room, slips her arms around you in a warm embrace, she communicates to you, "I don't want anything from you. I only want to show you that you are important to me and that I want to connect with you." The life-energy that comes from that benefits us both physically and emotionally.

I realize that for a variety of reasons, touch can be a sensitive topic. For some, there has been a great deal of woundedness in the area of sexual touch. So, while I am not ignoring the fact that sexual touch can also be an important and significant way to communicate treasuring, for our purposes here, I want to emphasize the essential nature of non-sexual touch in honoring your spouse. This must not be neglected. A study conducted by UCLA found that men and women need eight to ten meaningful touches every day in order to maintain both emotional and physical health.[7]

My mother-in-law recently commented to my wife that when she is with us, she notices that we are frequently holding hands or touching in small ways. This made me even more aware of what a neglected area this is in marriages. Shouldn't non-sexual physical connection with our mate be the norm instead of the exception? I encourage you to honor your mate with your touch.

6. Communicate

> When we fail to communicate openly and meaningfully—indeed, when we fail to share our lives with or mates—we dam up the stream of life and tend to create a stagnant pool of self-pity. We feel alone because we are alone. We may still live in the same house, but we live as two lonely people rather than as a unit.[8]

I don't imagine that there is any more important arena than communication when it comes to treasuring your mate. It is a subject about which a multitude of books have been written. Therefore, it would be futile to attempt to cover the subject with any great detail here. I want to use this brief space only to emphasize the critical nature of this subject and its importance to a complete and healthy marriage. Allow me to simply highlight some significant aspects of communication:

- Work for understanding and resolution. I can't tell you the number of times I hear couples frame their arguments in battle terms: They were "blindsided" or "ambushed." They weren't going to "give in," and they were determined to "win." When husbands and wives are more focused on winning the argument than they are on finding common ground, there will be no resolution in sight. Listen with the purpose of understanding your spouse.

- Use silence to allow thought, not to punish. As a child, I watched my dad sometimes go for weeks without so much as speaking a word to my mom. When he was mad at her, he would use silence to punish and manipulate her. This does nothing toward building bridges in a relationship. Instead, it confirms just how "stuck" and miserable you are.

- Say clearly what you mean instead of using all-or-nothing language. When people are upset and want to make a point, they will frequently make statements such as, "You always do that," "You never take care of things," "I hate football," and other over-the-top statements. If they were more honest in their words, they might instead say, "You seem to do that frequently," "You often fail to take care of things," or, "While I know that you enjoy watching football, I sometimes feel less important than the games. I wonder if we could spend some time together this weekend?" When we use extreme words to make a point, it creates defensiveness in our spouse and distance between us.

- Use "I" messages. In our culture of "somebody is to blame—and it's not me," we have become pretty adept at "you" messages: "You make me so mad" or, "I wouldn't have to get so angry if you hadn't done…" We know how to play the blame game well. However, when I use "I" messages, I take responsibility for my own feelings. While I may not like how you treated me, I own my reaction. So,

I might say, "I feel disrespected when I am telling you something that is important to me and you cut me off. I would appreciate it if you would wait until I have finished before changing the conversation." The simple formula for an "I" message is to say, "I feel _____ (an emotion) when you do _____ (a behavior), and I would ask that _____ (make a request—perhaps to stop the behavior, or if it's something you like, to continue it). Owning my own feelings helps to take away defensiveness and can lead to greater understanding and cooperation.

- Work toward resolution instead of simply a cease-fire. Too many times, we walk away from an argument angry and unsettled. We may think that we will talk about it later, but we don't. A couple of days go by, we think about resurrecting the issue, but we both seem in a good mood at the moment and we hate to ruin things by bringing up a difficult topic. As a result, the issue isn't resolved and we will probably argue about the same thing, or something similar, again in the future. The cease-fire felt better than arguing so we settled for it. Don't! Work toward actually resolving problems instead.

- Strive to communicate at all levels. The Rosbergs describe five levels of communication that grow in depth and richness—sharing 1) general information, 2) facts, 3) opinions and beliefs, 4) feelings and emotions, and 5) needs, intimate concerns, hope, and fears.[9] Many couples rarely venture past the first two on the list. Yet when we travel down this ever-deepening communication path, we begin to build bridges that will strengthen and energize our relationship.

- Ask for what you want. The Book of James says, "*...You do not have because you do not ask...*" (James 4:2). While James is specifically speaking about our relationship with God, there is a valuable principle here that is applicable to our relationships. Because we fear vulnerability, we are sometimes less than direct in communicating our desires. We may offer vague hints or ask confusing hidden-agenda questions. Sometimes we ask what I would call "set-up questions" that paint the other person into a corner—questions like, "Don't I always tell you that I love you?" This question is not really a question but a camouflage of one's true feelings. A more honest statement might be, "I am hurt because you just said that I never tell you that I love you." We will do far better if we can learn to state clearly our desires and ask for what we want from our spouse.

7. Change and Grow

"She's not the person I married," is often a statement spoken by a client who is unhappy that his wife has changed. Yet if someone were to ask us if we want our spouse to grow and develop, we would undoubtedly respond with, "Of course." What we probably mean by that is, "Of course, as long as it doesn't mess up my world or 'the way I think things ought to be.'"

The reality is that the person we married will most likely not be the person with whom we end our life. I am not talking here about ditching your spouse and finding someone else. My reference is to the fact that we all grow and change—which should be exciting.

I so appreciate Tim Keller's well-stated perspective on this. He says that when we fall in love, we "get a glimpse of the person God is creating," and we should say, "I see who God is making you, and it excites me! I want to be part of that. I want to partner with you and God in the journey you are taking to His throne. And when we get there, I will look at your magnificence and say, 'I always knew you could be like this. I got glimpses of it on earth, but now look at you!'"[10] What an amazing, unselfish, partnering picture. It says, "I absolutely value and treasure you." I want to be a part of that.

8. *Energize Each Other*

Becoming a source of strength and renewal for your mate is sometimes easy, sometimes fun, and sometimes…not so much. But this energizing can happen in a number of ways.

- It is essential that we learn to love even when it is difficult. It is not uncommon to make the mistake of thinking "difficult" is synonymous with "impossible." Labeling feelings as such only creates more emotional challenges. You see, "difficult" we can overcome. "Impossible" we can't. Challenges are not the same as failure. As the Lauers state, "It is important not to just observe the behavior of others, but to put a correct interpretation on it."[11]

- There is generally not a quick fix for problems in our marriage. In our world of easy gratification, we typically fail to view challenges as opportunities for growth. It is imperative that we give our relationships time so that they have the opportunity to become what God intended them to be.

- We need to keep moving forward. Not all marriages explode. Some slowly deteriorate until someone wakes up one day to the realization that the marriage is going "nowhere." That feels hopeless. Keep striving to take your marriage "somewhere."

- You probably have heard the phrase, "You are only as good as your last success." People will celebrate your accomplishment or victory today, but it is quickly forgotten if we don't continue to succeed. Similarly, in our marriages, reflecting on what we are doing well is important, but we should continue to strive to exceed what we have done and find new and creative ways to love our spouse.

- I have mentioned this before, but it is good to emphasize it again: feed your marriage a healthy dose of continual humor, playfulness, spontaneity, and creativity. Laugh more. This will have an unbelievable bonding effect in your relationship.

- Set goals together. Amos 3:3 says, *"Do two walk together unless they have agreed to do so?"* If my wife and I decide to go on vacation together, we must first talk about and agree upon our destination. Otherwise, the car will be loaded, the cooler will be stocked, and off we will head down I-25 until we reach New Mexico, only to discover that she thought we are going to California while I had Florida in mind. At this point a decision has to be made—either one of us must change our mind or we are going to need two separate cars. Similarly, making sure that we are on the same page in our relationship with God and our destination of eternity is critical to smooth travel. Also, working with our spouse to set goals together about everything from parenting issues to future retirement plans communicates, "You are my partner, and I choose to include you in my thinking and my plans in life because I value you."

If you want your marriage to be different than it is today, it will require first and foremost a change of heart. In order for your heart to change, the things you treasure will have to change. If you are like most, you may believe that you are more than willing to change but you are "certain" that your spouse isn't. I have no idea whether he or she is willing or not. But what I do know is this—you are the one reading this book. Therefore, the initial responsibility falls on you. What would happen if you began today to treasure your spouse in some of the ways listed in this chapter? Who knows? And no one will until you try.

In the book *No Longer Strangers*, Reverend Bruce Larson tells the story of a woman who complained that she and her husband no longer had much of a relationship:

> "Do you love him?" Larson asked. "Yes," she said as her eyes filled with tears. "But I'm sure that he doesn't love me, or he wouldn't be so cold and indifferent." The minister asked, "Why do you think he comes home every night instead of spending his time with someone else? Perhaps he's hoping that one day something will happen to rekindle the love you shared when you first married. What would be the worst thing that could happen if, after dinner, you put on something sexy and curled up beside him on the couch?" "He might laugh at me." A few days later the minister received a note from the wife: "Guess what? He didn't laugh."[12]

Why not give "treasuring" a try? As the woman in the story said, the worst your spouse could do is laugh. However, there is a good chance that he or she has feelings similar to yours. And if he or she does, the best that could happen might be renewed possibilities.

"There are many chapters in your life.
Don't get lost in the one you're in now."
—Unknown[1]

Chapter Eleven

Seasons of Change– Preparing For the Storm

It was a crisp January afternoon as the sun began its descent. Annie had completed last-minute conversations with the wedding coordinator while Doug nervously attempted to button his tuxedo shirt. Today was the day—the day that their little girl was getting married. This day had been a year in the making—well, actually, more like thirty years in the making. But during the previous twelve months, Annie and their daughter had been planning showers, shopping for dresses, tasting cakes, designing invitations—and the list went on. Doug watched all of this from afar, knowing that if he got too involved, he was liable to mess things up. After all, he had recently re-watched the movie *Father of the Bride*, and he did not want to be cast as George Banks, the father whose head nearly imploded from stress. Besides, he was amazed at what a masterful job Annie had done in navigating all the wedding details while keeping their daughter's feet somewhere near the ground.

The ceremony went without a hitch. And now with the reception in full swing, Annie and Doug both finally felt as though they could relax and breathe a little easier. Friends and family continually stopped by their table to express what a lovely wedding they had created and what a beautiful daughter they had raised. Doug squeezed Annie's hand as they exchanged grateful glances—grateful for all the work that had gone into this day, but more importantly, for all the efforts that had gone into their relationship. Today they were privileged to enjoy some of the benefits of those efforts.

Following the seemingly endless number of toasts that were offered to the bride and groom, they sipped their champagne and sat back, taking it all in. This was a moment that would be etched in their memories.

It was about then that a young couple, friends of their daughter's, came by and sat down to compliment them on a fabulous wedding and reception. However, what came next caught Doug and Annie off guard: the couple stated, "Your daughter is so lucky to have you two as parents. She has had such great role models to learn from, as you seem to have it all together. You are the perfect couple. We hope that we can have as strong of a marriage as you do. What is your secret? How can we have what you have?"

In that brief moment, before they responded, a wave of emotions washed over them. They knew how close they had come to not making it. While they had learned lessons that had enabled them to infuse life into a relationship that had not always been easy, this young couple did not need to know all of that. Yet they were being asked a terrific question. What could they share with two people who were in the early stages of their journey? What advice could they offer that would prepare them for the years ahead?

Doug thought for a moment and then replied, "As our daughter has told us, you two have been married a few months. You are newlyweds with a clean canvas upon which you are beginning to paint.

Enjoy this time, because it is a precious season. But be aware that just like the turning of the pages of the calendar, you will experience changing seasons—spring, summer, fall, winter, and nuances of everything in between. Right now the sun is bright and the breezes are invigorating. But know that there will be cold temperatures and high winds. There will be storms—I assure you. Yet there is no need to fear the storms if you will prepare for them. Therein lies our advice. You will experience many different seasons in your marriage—prepare for them, embrace each other through them, and then enjoy them."

Black Forest

On June 11, 2013, at approximately one o'clock in the afternoon, the most destructive fire to date in Colorado history began. By the time the fire was one hundred percent contained, it had burned 14,200 acres, destroyed 509 homes, and resulted in the loss of two lives. Over 13,000 homes and 38,000 people were evacuated. While this fire was devastating all by itself, what made it more emotionally complicating was the fact that it came almost exactly a year after the Waldo Canyon fire, also in Colorado Springs. The community was still recovering and rebuilding from the previous year when two lives were lost, along with 346 homes.

Depending on your age, you may remember exactly where you were when you heard that President Kennedy was shot, or when you saw the Challenger Space Shuttle explode, or when you witnessed the image of the commercial airliner flying into the Twin Towers on 9/11 flash across the television screen. Similarly, I remember coming out of Home Depot on that Tuesday afternoon in June 2012 as the Waldo Canyon fire erupted over the mountain ridge and headed down into Colorado Springs. The smoke was so thick and dark even twenty miles away that street lights were coming on at four o'clock in the afternoon, tricked into thinking it was nighttime.

Living in the Colorado Springs area, my wife and I have good friends who lost their homes in one or the other of these two fires. We have seen the toll that the loss of a lifetime of memories has taken on both individuals and families. As I write this, some are still rebuilding.

Investigators of these fires have pointed out two significant contributors to the rapid spread of the blazes. The first factor reported by officials was the lack of awareness of risks, while the second was not preparing for those risks of which they were aware. Most of the homes in the Black Forest area were on plots of five acres or more, many of them heavily wooded. It is certainly a beautiful setting, but with it come inherent risks. Recognizing those risks should lead individuals to minimize them. While mitigation may have not made a difference in some instances, one homeowner noted that his property and some of those adjacent to his were better mitigated than others. This resulted in reduced fire intensity, and as he related, it "stopped the fire 100 feet from my house."[2]

Following the Waldo Canyon fire, the Colorado Springs fire marshal reported that the area was recovering quickly. However, he stated that while the neighborhood's mitigation efforts had become a model for other cities, it did not always take into account the danger of certain zones. When an area is wiped out, it makes "room for bigger, more expensive dream homes in zones that remain a risk for wildfire."[3]

While I have taken a somewhat lengthy look at the devastation caused by and the contributors to these two fires, it is not without reason. It is clearly evident that homeowners need to be aware of risks, mitigate to reduce risks, and work to not build in risky terrain. Similar truths are relevant to our marriages.

Couple after couple enters marriage with the naïve thought that "I love you; you love me—this will be easy and perfect." Never mind that it hasn't been for anyone else. They begin their journey without having taken stock of the dangers that they are certain to encounter.

On the other hand, some start down the marital path well aware of the pitfalls that lay ahead. They have seen others struggle, and they know that it will not be easy. Yet like some of those living in heavily wooded forests, they do no mitigation work, no preparation. So, when the marriage comes under fire, they are in danger of losing a lifetime of memories.

While some devastated by a failed marriage gain valuable insight and learn to do relationships differently, others recover quickly. They clear the marriage path, much like the burned home, and rebuild with haste. No emotional healing has taken place; no new relational insights have been implemented. They simply rebuild quickly to medicate their pain of being alone. When these are the steps taken, devastation from the next wildfire may be just over the horizon.

Charley, Frances, Ivan, and Jeanne

In his book *The Heart of Commitment,* Scott Stanley discusses the need for couples to invest in their relationship for the long term. In doing so, they build up what he calls "relationship capital."[4] This concept accounts for those couples who are intentional about investing in, as well as protecting, each other and the relationship. Naïvely believing that having strong loving feelings for one another is enough to weather the difficulties of life will result in a path lined with carnage. Building and strengthening your relationship during the good times is essential to weathering the bad. When couples are faced with a crisis in their marriage, they typically either fall apart or hunker down and draw close together. As Stanley says, "The ones who draw together are the ones who have built up some capital in their marriage. They have something to draw upon."[5]

In 2004, the State of Florida experienced something that hadn't happened in 120 years. During a six-week period, four major hurricanes—Charley, Frances, Ivan, and Jeanne—pounded the state. Combined, these hurricanes caused more than $20 billion in damages and left more than 2.3 million residents without power. The Federal Emergency Management Agency (FEMA) responded with 11,000 workers, fourteen million meals, and 10.8 million gallons of water. While 128 lives were lost, authorities knew that it could have been far worse. Yet it wasn't, because of the preparations that had been made.[6]

The same could not be said for New Orleans when, in August 2005, Hurricane Katrina, a Category 5 storm, ripped through the city. While this was an unbelievably powerful storm, in many ways it was one of the "most anticipated natural disaster[s] in modern American history."[7] Certainly, hurricanes are not new to the Gulf Coast, as nearly twenty percent of all hurricanes hitting the United States between 1851 and 2004 have landed in Louisiana.[8] But New Orleans is particularly vulnerable. It sits at an average of six feet below sea level. A series of levees surround the city for protection, but they have had a troubled history. Pumps have been designed to siphon water out of these low-lying areas, which works under normal circumstances. However, in the event of a major storm, the pumps are unable to function when they are submerged by overwhelming volumes of water.

Having relatives in Louisiana, I remember well the destruction that the state experienced as a result of Hurricane Camille in 1969. As storms would brew during hurricane season and head toward the Louisiana coast, my cousins, along with other residents, would sit on pins and needles, waiting to see what was going to happen. I recall images of families scrambling to procure water and supplies, boarding up homes and businesses, and attempting to evacuate the area. But as many would attest, those are survival reactions to a crisis but a far cry from adequate preparation.

This same principle is accurately pictured in our marriages. I receive phone calls weekly from couples in crisis. Rarely do they call me as minor cracks begin to appear in the relationship. Instead, they do their best to ignore the warning signs of oncoming danger. Resisting the admission that they are in serious trouble, they operate as though ignoring the problems will keep them from existing. So, when I finally get the call, their relationship is hanging over a 5,000-foot drop-off, with three fingernails clinging to the edge of the cliff. This troubling scene has been repeated hundreds of thousands of times in the lives of married couples. Similar to Hurricane Katrina, these marriages could be termed "the most anticipated of marital disasters."

The time to reinforce levees and design better protective systems is when the weather is warm, the sun is shining, and the winds are calm. To decide to do these things when the storm is barreling down the coastline is too late—and the results can be destructive, resulting in loss of life. Likewise, the time to prepare our marriages for the inevitable trials of life is when the interactions are easy, the love is strong, and the relationship is glowing. To wait until tempers are flaring and cooperation is in short supply can be calamitous, resulting in the tragic loss of marital life.

Yet couple after couple recounts stories of unresolved conflict that is perpetuated in their relationship. They know that solutions haven't been found to problems, but rather than bring them up for constructive discussion, they gloss over them for fear of rocking the boat. The thinking goes something like, "Well, he seems in a good mood today. I know that we need to talk about that issue from last night, but I am afraid to upset the applecart. Maybe if I just don't say anything, we will get along okay." And sometimes they do—for that day. But the conflict that will arise from these unresolved issues is more predictable than the weather. It is essential that we learn to engage in difficult conversations with our spouse during the relational sunshine and not wait for the storms.

Seasons of Change

As I have mentioned earlier in this book, one of the greatest certainties about marriage is that things are going to change. The person that you marry at twenty-five is not the same person with whom you will celebrate your fiftieth wedding anniversary. Oh yes, your spouse will still have the same name, birthdate, and Social Security number, but the person he or she has grown to be will greatly differ from whom he or she was when the journey began. During your marriage, you will progress through a number of seasons with lots of transitions. I appreciate the way that authors Pam and Bill Farrel put it when they write, "Marriages are made or broken in the transitions of life. Between the transition points, most relationships operate smoothly. It's the change points that test us."[9]

Consider the seasons or stages of life that you have experienced with your mate. Most remember those early days of being "newlyweds." Everything is fresh, new, and exciting. It is easy to take this season for granted, believing that marriage will always be this easy. Yet this is one of those "warm weather times." People refer to this as "the honeymoon period." They may say things like, "Look how in love they are. Wait until the honeymoon is over." While the initial stages of a new marriage may indeed be easier than other stages, rest assured that changes will be coming.

Therefore, I encourage couples in this season to take advantage of all that it offers. Use this time to build healthy patterns of interaction. These may include having a regular date night, praying together daily, and growing and learning together sexually—connecting intimately on a regular basis. This is an important time for constructing levees and systems around "we." From our earliest memories, we have focused on "me", learning to blame and deflect responsibility. As we encounter stress and conflict in our marriage, we can easily become masters of "me." But if we do, it can contribute to our undoing.

There is power in "we," and this is the season to learn it. It will be invaluable later.

For some, this bonding time before children can last for years. For others, it can be as short-lived as nine months from the wedding night. But regardless of the length of time, if children are on the horizon, a new season will commence. Time will seem to be constantly "hurried." Those lazy Saturday mornings of sleeping in will quickly become a distant memory. Some sociologists use the term "parenting crisis" to refer to this time when our serene little world has chaos thrust upon it. Schedules are stretched at the seams by a myriad of sports and other extracurricular pursuits by our children. We attempt to maintain a precarious balance between our careers, our families, personal relationships, and time with our mate. It can feel simply overwhelming.

Compared to this stage, the newlywed period will feel like a cake-walk. If we were intentional in our pattern building during the first season, this one will weather the pace better. However, if we failed to brace for the storm when it was sunny, then this "hurry up" season will be more challenging.

During this season, I want to encourage you to be very intentional about the following practices: carving out twenty to thirty minutes a day to connect outside of the earshot of the kids, while acknowledging that time is a luxury; making date night with your spouse a priority; and planning to do something specifically for your marriage at least once a year. This could be a vacation without the kids or perhaps a marriage retreat of some kind. Remember—ideally, marriage retreats are not for those "poor souls" whose marriages are on the brink of death. They are as critical to the sustainability of a healthy marriage as regular check-ups are to the longevity of the life of your car. Two other items I would add here—read books together with your spouse that will grow your marriage, and pray for and with each other frequently.

Progressing from the "hurried season" to what is often referred to as "midlife" may require all the strength we can muster. Depending on if and when you had children, you could still have young ones at home, or they may have graduated and be away at college. You may be actively engaged in parenting or learning to write a new chapter as "empty nesters." Teenagers who vaguely remind you of the children you brought home from the hospital may live in your house. They may be masters of dividing you and your spouse—working to pit you against each other in order to keep the heat off themselves. Or they may be working toward that college degree, siphoning off every dollar you are willing to make available.

As you steer through this season, it is critical that you cling to each other. Whether it is for survival, as you work to keep the kids from ganging up on you, or whether it is for reacquainting yourselves with each other, cling and cling tightly. Again, there is no substitute for making time for each other. Recognizing that you have responsibilities that range from being role models for your children to taking care of aging parents is essential. As a couple, you need to be a rock of support and comradery for all the demands you are facing. You need each other! I encourage you to talk on a regular basis about things that matter, including how to approach challenges as a united front and what each of you needs in order to feel that you have an unwavering partner.

Finally, whether they are called "the golden", "retirement," or "the legacy years," this stage marks the latter part of your journey together. You will have more time for each other, which, in one sense, may make this the richest season yet. It is a time of mentoring others as well as passing on your legacy to your kids and grandkids. Enjoy the fullness of this final chapter together. If you have fed the relationship appropriately during the previous seasons, this one can be extremely satisfying.

As the Farrels state, "You can't always foresee the changes that will affect your marriage, but you always have a choice in whether those transitions make you resilient or make you want to run."[10] In each of these stages, repeatedly practicing the skills that connect you could very well determine the sustainability of your marriage.

Lee Yoon-Hye, a flight attendant with Asiana Airlines, knows exactly how true the need for practice is. On July 6, 2013, Flight 214, on its way from South Korea, crashed just short of the runway at San Francisco International Airport. Striking the ground and a seawall, three flight attendants were ejected. Lee and her colleagues assisted hundreds of passengers in getting out of the wreck safely. When the emergency slide trapped passengers, Lee passed a knife to the copilot to puncture the slide. As flames erupted, she tossed a fire extinguisher to a colleague. She indicated that she didn't really give things a lot of thought; she just followed her training and did what needed to be done—all while she unknowingly had a broken tailbone.[11]

She discovered what scientists have known for years—that when you practice something over and over again, the responsibility for the action is shifted from the conscious part of the brain to the other parts that operate automatically. Similarly, as we engage in intentional strategies during the various seasons of our marriage, repeatedly practicing skills that work, we are preparing ourselves for those times when stress and fear might otherwise paralyze us. Rather than withdraw and shut down, we are better prepared to tackle the challenges that come our way. But we have to prepare.

Whether we perform fire mitigation on our wooded property, execute levee repairs in hurricane country, actively train for commercial airline work, or engage in this journey called marriage, necessary and appropriate preparation can save our existence.

Stay the Course

As important as practice and preparation are to the solidarity of our marriages, we live in a culture that shies away from discipline and hard relational work. Instead we hear a steady stream of, "Do what makes you happy today." Rather than the exercising of patience and wisdom, society encourages spontaneity and fun. There is no need to experience heartache, pain, sadness, or loss. Instead, we are advised to take a pill, find a new relationship, and just "go with the flow." "Intentionality"—that sounds so boring and stifling. "I need to be free, be myself, and do what I need to do—for me." Yet these various philosophies that clamor for our attention, promising a guilt-free, pain-free, fun-filled life, actually deliver death—the death of our integrity, the destruction of our relationships, and the demise of who we were called to be.

According to Greek mythology, there once were creatures known as Sirens. These beings were believed to be incredibly beautiful and enticing. Appearing as a mixture of both female and bird characteristics, they lured sailors to their death by singing songs that were irresistibly sad and sweet, resulting in sailors crashing their ships into the rocks.

It is said that Odysseus was curious as to what the Sirens sang and wanted to hear their song. Of course, he knew that if he were to do that, it most certainly would mean his demise. Therefore, he devised a plan. He had all his sailors plug their ears with beeswax so that they could not hear the song. Then they were to tie him to the mast. He ordered them to leave him tightly tied regardless of what he screamed, ordered, or begged. As he heard the captivating song, he ordered his sailors to untie him but instead they bound him tighter. It was only after they were out of earshot that he was released.[12]

In a culture that values beauty over substance and happiness over holiness, we at times must tie ourselves to the mast and/or plug our ears. If we are to be what Scripture calls *"a chosen people, a royal priesthood, a holy nation,* [a] *people* [belonging] *to God,"* then we must take a different approach than that which is taken by society (1 Peter 2:9 GW). It is incumbent on us to become men and women who prepare for the storm. In our marriages, we are certain to encounter trouble. Don't misunderstand me—I am not saying it is likely; I am clearly stating that it is certain. It's during the transition times, when the waves are turbulent and are pulling people apart, that we have to hold on to each other even more tightly. Our ability to navigate these moments will be linked directly to how well we have prepared. If you are in the newlywed stage, commit yourself to preparation through each and every season. If you are in a later stage and are feeling disillusioned and stuck, commit yourself to reengagement and preparation in whatever season you find yourself. It is not too late. He who began a good work in you will be faithful to complete it—if you allow Him to work unrestricted in your life (see Phil. 1:6).

"In the end, we won't remember the most beautiful face and body. We'll remember the most beautiful heart and soul."
—Karen Salmansohn[1]

CHAPTER TWELVE

Remembering

"What a sight!" Annie exclaimed. Doug responded, "Better than I deserve." Annie turned to look at him and found him staring at her. "No, not me—the sunset, you goofball." "Oh yeah, that's not bad either," he said. They were sitting on their balcony, basking in the sun, while the smell of the ocean relaxed them with each breath. This was their second trip to Hawaii, and they were thoroughly enjoying their time together.

As they reclined on this lazy afternoon, they permitted their thoughts and memories to run free. Doug recalled what he liked to refer to as "the ambush"—when Annie first expressed her interest in Doug. He always tried to play like he was an innocent victim who didn't have a chance. But the reality was he had been equally interested in this attractive young lady. She noted how impressed she had been when they were walking downtown and he made it a point to walk on the street-side of the sidewalk as her dad had done with her mom. She had never known another man to do that. He shared with her how moved he had been when she counted him her friend first and foremost.

unstuck

As the hours crept by, they talked. They talked about the early years of their marriage, the challenging times, the days when they really believed they might not make it, and more importantly, the day they knew that they absolutely would. It was good to remember.

They remembered the beginning of one spring vacation when they were stuck on the interstate for two hours in a snow storm that they weren't sure they were going get out of. They laughed as they recalled how they almost went to the bathroom on the side of the freeway. They recounted how difficult it had been to lose their dads and the challenges of moving on in life without them. Doug reminisced about the support Annie always offered when he launched some new career venture. Her encouragement allowed him to take calculated risks, knowing that she was in his court. Annie expressed the significance of his unwavering faith in her when she faced an unexpected career shift and her self-worth had taken a serious hit.

After returning home from their vacation, they had dinner with their daughter and her husband. During the meal, their daughter asked, "So what was your favorite part of the trip? Was it seeing the active volcano, visiting the coffee farms, walking along the beach, going to the luau? What did you most enjoy?" Doug thought for a minute and said, "All those things were fun. We had a great time tasting coffee, watching the luau dancers, and, of course, we absolutely loved hanging out on the beach. But I would have to say that my favorite thing out of the entire week there was simply being with your mom, remembering all that we have shared and pondering how we want to love each other every moment for the rest of our days—and then some." Playfully, their daughter said, "Ah, how sweet." Then she acted as though she was going to be sick. "I know—sounds kind of sappy," Doug replied. "But it is absolutely true!"

Annie had been quiet while Doug spoke. But now she interjected: "You know, I couldn't agree with your dad more. While I enjoyed lounging around and reading and being able to sleep in, I most enjoyed just being, remembering, and then planning some more life together. I think that is part of what makes us stronger." When her son-in-law expressed confusion, saying, "I'm not sure I understand," Annie replied, "It is so easy to be distracted by what goes wrong that we often forget to focus on what has gone right. We forget about the things we have struggled to successfully overcome together. We minimize the impact of tender moments together and the ways that our partnering as a couple has made us more resilient individually. By recounting the realities of our history together, we strengthen our marriage. By hearing the words spoken out loud, we are reassured of the truth of these events." And then Doug added, "And by retelling the stories to you, our love is witnessed, confirmed, and passed on—for our benefit as well as for yours."

Don't Rewrite History

With regularity I listen as couples tell me how they have never trusted their spouse, never been happy with them, and aren't even certain that they ever really loved them. However, if I am able to get an account of their life—whether from their spouses, friends, or family—I typically will get a more complete picture. Couples who have been wounded by each other over time frequently engage in what I call "revisionist history." One such couple sat in my office this past month doing exactly that.

With their marriage crashing against the rocks, David and Trina called for an appointment. Their marriage had almost gone sideways a few years earlier, but David had realized some mistakes he had made and proclaimed a renewed love and dedication to his wife. Best of all, he backed it up with action. But here they were two years later with David having been caught in an extramarital affair. They were in serious trouble. While I would like to say that David really figured it out this time, acknowledged his grave error, and deeply repented to his wife, that is not what happened. Instead, he said that it was all her fault. He began by narrating how she had flirted with a man at a business party about ten years ago. While a big argument had ensued at the time, he had recognized that it was an unintentional wound on her part, and they worked through it.

Yet now, ten years later, that event had taken on a significance previously unseen. What was actually happening was "revisionist history." Whether it was because he had forgotten how well they had mended things and how much love he had felt for his wife then, or whether it was because revising history served his purposes to justify behavior now, the results were the same. He was working to create a new version of reality.

It is *especially* at the low times of a marriage that an accurate recollection is important. It is highly unlikely that we would marry someone because we never liked them in the first place, we couldn't trust them, and we thought they were ugly. If that were true, then we needed some intense therapy back then. Recalling the positives that led to our marrying each other is needed during the difficult times. When things are bad, we have a tendency to rewrite history and convince ourselves that things have never been good so we had better get out of this awful marriage. I hear individuals say, "I don't love him anymore. As a matter of fact, I'm not sure I ever did." This is revisionist history on display.

Remembering the positives in our relationship is essential to our marital health and our commitment to one another. If reengagement is to have a chance, we have to remember the real story.

Shema Yisrael

Shema is the Hebrew word that is often used in the Torah to refer to daily Jewish prayers. Specifically, *Shema* means "listen" or "hear," and it begins an important section of Scripture for the Jewish people. In Deuteronomy 6:4-9 a command begins that says:

> *Hear, O Israel: The Lord our God, the Lord is One. Love the Lord your God with all your heart and with all your*

soul and with all your strength. These commandments that I give you today are to be upon your hearts. Impress them on your children. Talk about them when you sit at home and when you walk along the road, when you lie down and when you get up. Tie them as symbols on your hands and bind them on your foreheads. Write them on the doorframes of your houses and on your gates (Deuteronomy 6:4-9).

This is a passage about remembering. The Lord our God knows how quickly and easily we will forget what He has done for us, how He sustains us, and how desperately we need Him. In some orthodox circles of Judaism you will still see the tying of symbols on the hands and foreheads and garments. Many Jewish homes will affix a mezuzah to the door frame of their house. This is a piece of parchment usually contained in a small attractive case, which is inscribed with these verses from Deuteronomy. Some will mount a mezuzah on every door frame inside the house as well. It is believed that the body of commands to which this passage refers are the 613 commands in the Torah that are referred to as the "mitzvot."

As we read further in this chapter in Deuteronomy, we see continued reminders. Verses 10-12 talk about how easy it is to forget God when things are going well. The passage says that when God's people made it to the Promised Land and found themselves with houses, plenty of food, prolific vineyards, and all kinds of good things, they were likely to become satisfied, forgetting that it was God who brought them there, gave them the land, and provided for them (see Deut. 6:10-12).

Later in the chapter, instructions are given about talking with their children. Verse 20 begins: *"In the future, when your son asks you, 'What is the meaning of…'"* (Deuteronomy 6:20). The passage then refers to God's laws and decrees and says that this was the time to explain to their children all that God had done for His people, beginning with the time that He led them out of Egypt (see Deut. 6:20-25).

You see, God was trying to get His people to remember what was important. Was the passage stating that wearing things on our clothes, displaying symbols on our person or our homes is what is most significant? Probably not. It is easy to get hung up on having something mounted on the door frame and really have no idea what God's commands and desires are. The issue of importance here was and is—remembering. God was using the symbols to help anchor those memories in their hearts. If we remember all the blessings that have come from God and the ways He has empowered us to live, we will bless Him by our faithful obedience and service. But if we forget, then we start to think that we have done this ourselves—that we have pulled ourselves up by our bootstraps and that we don't need anybody. We naïvely think that we have what we have because of our own self-sufficiency. When we do that, we act as though there is no God and simply do what we think is right in our own eyes.

We see throughout Scripture that when this happened, God's people were in chaos, were captured by other nations, and lost all of their possessions. God essentially was saying in this passage, "Remember who I am, what I have done for you, and how I have provided for you. If you do, you will love Me with all your heart, soul, and strength. You will be passionate about obeying My commands and pursuing a relationship with Me. As a result, your life will have meaning, purpose, and fulfillment. If you do not, you will experience fear, anxiety, and a sense of lostness that will overwhelm you" (see Deut. 6:1-25).

God knows the necessity of remembering to ensuring our relationship with Him is vibrant and healthy. It is my desire that the significance of this concept and its applicability to our marriages not be lost here. "Revisionist history," which was discussed earlier, is a direct result of not remembering. Forgetting that we were once thrilled to simply hang out together nonstop is due to the fact that we have not been intentional about remembering. Remembering is essential.

God emphasized the importance of symbols and other concrete reminders to an accurate memory. He even said that there will come a time when our children will ask us about them, providing us with an opportunity to retell the story of what God has done for us (see Deut. 6:20-25). And in doing so, we pass on the memories to our children and hopefully to their children. The passage says when we are walking, when we are going to bed, or even when we are speaking first thing in the morning—whenever—we are to talk about what God has done and is doing in our lives. It is that important—more than anything!

I recently watched a video clip of interviews with university students. Consistently, students couldn't answer basic history questions: who won the civil war? when did America achieve independence? or even, who currently sits as the vice president? Yet without much hesitation, these same students knew the wives of Brad Pitt, shows in which celebrities starred, and the names of popular musical artists. How sad this is. But even more startling is that we would know this trivia and somehow fail to know the truly important ways that God has intervened in our history and in our lives.

Think of the power that these interactions hold. Imagine that your children ask you about a particular picture of you and your spouse that you have hanging on a wall, or that they inquire as to why celebrating your anniversary is so vital to you. Maybe they wonder about the importance of a particular gift that was given to you by your spouse. Or perhaps they want to know about the significance of your wedding rings. There it is—the opportunity to tell your story of love, the chance to pass on the heritage of a loving relationship. You are being given a powerful tool to model love for your children. They will learn by watching—not so much by how you treat a symbol, but by how that symbol reminds you and leads to the expression of undying love for your mate. In turn, they learn from you how to faithfully love and serve their future mate.

Listen Up

"Shema"—"Hear"—"O Israel..." (Deuteronomy 6:4). The Scriptures are saying, "Listen up. I am going to tell you some undeniable truths about the living God." Similarly, I want to encourage you: "Listen up, those of you in a marital relationship. There are important things to remember about the relationship with your mate. I want you to give him or her gifts on your anniversary. I want you to wear a ring as a symbol of your singular commitment to your spouse. And when your kids ask you about why you married their mother or father, I want you to tell them the story. Tell it and retell it. When you are walking or driving, camping out, or eating lunch, tell them about why you share your life with their other parent. Do it because it is that important!

Still, you may be saying to yourself, "Okay, I get that recalling the way things were with some accuracy is important. But it has been so long since we recaptured any fond memories, I'm not even sure where to begin. How do I start?" Let me suggest some easy, practical tips.

1) Utilize photos and videos. I love pictures. Maybe it is because I am a visual person, but I take pictures, print them out, and put them in albums. Yes, that's right—I put real pictures in real albums. They are not just saved in my phone or on the computer. I can actually hold them in my hands. I video Christmases and birthdays and significant events and watch and re-watch them over the years. It anchors the veracity of the event.

2) Tell and retell the stories of your meeting, your dating, your wedding—anything about your relationship that you can. Do this every opportunity to whoever will listen—couples, friends, parents, kids, and grandkids. We are so quick to tell them negatives about our spouse but not so quick to pass on the positives.

3) Practice the art of traditions—things you put into place and do with regularity as a couple that celebrate and mark occasions. For example, perhaps every anniversary you re-watch your wedding video, or maybe you relive your first date by going to the same restaurant and talking about what drew you to each other. The list of possibilities is endless.

4) Focus—this is the greatest protection you can have in any marriage. It is easy to forget the things that have lost your interest. But making it a point to think about and give attention to various aspects of your marriage will assist your heart in following your head's lead. If you are one who is prone to distraction and tend to forget significant dates, then put them in a calendar or write sticky notes to yourself. I sometimes hear people say that if you have to schedule it, then that means it is not important enough to you, or else you would remember. I would contend the exact opposite. If it is so important to you that you want to guarantee that you won't forget it, schedule it and write it down.

Throughout Scripture, in both the Old and New Testaments, we see God's emphasis on remembering. He creates concrete anchors for our memories because He knows that without them, we will forget. And if we forget, we lose sight of what this thing called "marriage" is all about.

Decide

Remembering why we married is essential if we are to get unstuck and stay unstuck. You see, the message of this book is that merely enduring, just somehow making our relationships limp pathetically along, is not good enough. We have been called to a much higher level of relational functioning—to a level of commitment that reflects the quality of a sacrificial love that God offers to each of us. But it requires intentionality.

In the course of the latter chapters of this book, we have examined the need to place God at the center of our heart, our life, and our marriage; learning how to address past hurts and future expectations; truly finding ways to begin a brand new way of dancing, of relating to our spouse; identifying critical steps required to begin once again to treasure and cherish our husband or wife; preparing for the seasons of change that we inevitably will encounter over the years of our marriage; and finally, identifying ways to solidly anchor the threads of our history and our story. All these things are directed toward creating vibrancy, health, hope, and life. But they won't be created by just reading the words on these pages. That is only the start. They will only take flight by acting upon them.

I want to end our literary journey together with a fitting story. Gary and Barbara Rosberg relate a powerful encounter experienced by a friend:

> While waiting to pick up a friend at the Portland, Oregon, airport, I had one of those life-changing experiences that you hear other people talk about—the kind that sneaks up on you unexpectedly. This one occurred merely two feet from me.

Straining to locate my friend coming off the jetway, I noticed a man coming toward me. He stopped right next to me to greet his family. First, he motioned to his younger son (about six years old) as he laid down his bags. They gave each other a long, loving hug. As they separated enough to look into each other's face, I heard the father say, "It's so good to see you, Son, I missed you so much!" His son smiled somewhat shyly, averted his eyes, and replied softly, "Me too, Dad!"

> Then the man stood up, gazed into the eyes of his older son (about nine), and while cupping his son's face in his hands, he said, "You're already quite the young man. I love you very much, Zach!" They too hugged a most loving, tender hug.

While this was happening, a toddler (about two years old) was squirming in her mom's arms, never once taking her eyes off her dad. The man said, "Hi, baby girl!" as he gently took the child from her mother. He kissed her face all over and then held her close to his chest while rocking her from side to side. The little girl instantly relaxed and simply laid her head on his shoulder, motionless in pure contentment.

After several moments he handed his daughter to his older son and declared, "I've saved the best for last," and proceeded to give his wife the longest, most passionate kiss I've ever seen. He gazed into her eyes for several seconds and then silently mouthed, "I love you so much!" They gazed into each other's eyes, beaming big smiles at one another, while holding both hands. For an instant they reminded me of newlyweds, but I knew by the age of their kids that they couldn't possibly be.

I puzzled about it for a moment then realized how totally engrossed I was in the wonderful display of love not more than an arm's length away from me. I suddenly felt uncomfortable, as if I were invading something sacred. I was amazed to hear my own voice nervously ask, "Wow! How long have you two been married?"

"Been together fourteen years total, married twelve of those," he replied without breaking the gaze from his wife's face.

"Well, then, how long have you been away?" I asked. The man finally turned and looked at me, still beaming his joyous smile. "Two whole days!"

"Two days?" I said, stunned. By the intensity of the greeting, I had assumed he had been gone for at least several weeks, if not months.

Wanting to end my intrusion, I said, "I hope my marriage is still that passionate after twelve years!"

The man suddenly stopped smiling. He looked me straight in the eye with a force that burned right into my soul. Then he told me something that left me a different person. He simply said, "Don't hope, friend. Decide!"

He flashed his wonderful smile again, shook my hand, and said, "God bless!" With that, he and his family turned and strolled away together.

I was still watching that exceptional man and his family walk out of sight when my friend came up to me and asked, "What are you looking at?"

Without hesitating, and with a curious sense of certainty, I replied, "My future!"[2]

No one gets married with the goal of being stuck. None of us planned to find ourselves one day contemplating divorce and the unraveling of our family. But neither are we thrilled by the idea of enduring a miserable relationship for the remainder of our days. My encouragement, my hope, and my prayers are that you will embrace the possibilities that come with a commitment to getting unstuck. It is not some "pie in the sky" fairytale. You don't have to remain stuck in the past, in what has been. Moving your marriage forward could be your "future." It really can happen. But remember the words of the dad above: "Don't hope, friend. Decide!"

Appendix

The complete list of interview questions that were used with the couples in chapter six are listed below.

1. How long have you been married?

2. How did you meet?

3. How long did you date before you were married?

4. Give an example of a difficult situation that you had to overcome as a couple that required intentional focus.

5. What steps did you take to address this, and what was the process for resolving or making significant progress towards resolution?

6. What has been the most challenging season of your marriage?

7. What have been the most rewarding aspects of your relationship?

8. What factors have you learned are the most important for a vibrant marriage?

9. How many children do you have?

10. What were the biggest challenges you faced as parents together, and how did you successfully address them?

11. Can you tell me about any challenges you have faced with regard to parents, in-laws, or siblings and how you have successfully navigated them?

12. What advice would you give young newlyweds who want the best chance at a successful and happy marriage?

13. What tips would you give to couples who are feeling stuck and without hope?

14. What else would you like for me to know?

Notes

1. *SearchQuotes*, accessed September 4, 2015, http://www.searchquotes.com/quotation/just_because-the-past-didn't-turn-out-like-you-wanted-it-to-doesn't-mean-your-future-can't-be-bette/534384/.

2. David M. Schnarch, *Constructing The Sexual Crucible: An Integration of Sexual and Marital Therapy* (New York, NY: W.W. Norton & Company, 1991), 296.

Chapter One

1. "Zig Ziglar Quotes," *BrainyQuote*, accessed September 4, 2015, http://www.brainyquote.com/quotes/quotes/z/zigziglar617764.html.

Chapter Two

1. "Quotes About Marriage to Inspire Love!" *The Intimate Couple*, accessed September 4, 2015, http://www.the-intimate-couple.com/quotes-about-marriage.html.

2. Tim Keller, *The Meaning of Marriage: Facing the Complexities of Commitment with the Wisdom of God* (New York, NY: Penguin Group, 2011), 26.

3. Scott Stanley, *The Heart of Commitment: Cultivating Lifelong Devotion in Marriage* (Nashville, TN: Thomas Nelson, 1998), 9.

4. Mike and Harriet McManus, *Living Together: Myths, Risks & Answers* (Brentwood, TN: Howard Books, 2008), 9.

5. Jeanette and Robert Lauer, *'Til Death Do Us Part: How Couples Stay Together* (New York, NY: The Haworth Press, 1986), 10.

Chapter Three

1. "Iz Quotes," accessed September 4, 2015, http://izquotes.com/quotes/?q=a+bizarre+sensation+pervades+a+relationship&t=1.

2. Tomas Jivanda, "Malaysia Airlines flight MH370: Stricken plane was 'thrown around like a fighter jet in attempt to dodge radar'," *The Independent*, April 13, 2014, accessed September 4, 2015, http://www.independent.co.uk/news/world/asia/missing-malaysia-airlines-flight-was-thrown-around-like-a-fighter-jet-after-disappearing-from-radar-9257368.html.

Chapter Four

1. *Quotes.com*, accessed September 4, 2015, http://16quotes.com/a-relationship-is-like-a-house/.

2. "Resign," *Dictionary.com*, accessed September 4, 2015, http://dictionary.reference.com/browse/resign?s=t.

3. "Extramarital Affairs." *Princess Diana: Affairs & Divorce*, accessed September 4, 2015, www.britishroyals.info/diana/biography6.html.

4. "Timeline: The Life of Diana, Princess of Wales," *CBSNews.com*, August 24, 2012, accessed September 4, 2014, http://www.cbsnews.com/media/timeline-the-life-of-diana-princess-of-wales/21/.

5. John Hall, "Revealed: Marilyn Monroe called Jackie Kennedy to confess affair with 'drug addict' JFK and was told, 'that's great, I'll move out and you have all the problems'," *The Independent,* August 5, 2013, accessed September 4, 2015, www.independent.co.uk/news/world/americas/revealed-marilyn-monroe-called-jackie-kennedy-to-confess-to-affair-with-drug-addict-jfk-and-was-told-thats-great-ill-move-out-and-you-have-all-the-problems-8746177.html.

Chapter Five

1. *Idlehearts,* accessed September 4, 2014, http://www.idlehearts.com/29250/marriage-does-not-guarantee-you-will-be-together-forever.

2. Gary and Barbara Rosberg, *Divorce-Proof Your Marriage* (Wheaton, IL: Tyndale House Publishers, 2002), 6.

3. "Commitment," *Dictionary.com,* accessed September 4, 2015, http://dictionary.reference.com/browse/commitment?s=t.

4. Gay and Kathlyn Hendricks, *Conscious Loving: The Journey to Co-Commitment* (New York, NY: Bantam Books, 1990), 11.

5. Keller, 29.

6. Ibid., 34.

7. Stanley, xiii.

8. Linda and Charlie Bloom, *101 Things I Wish I Knew When I Got Married: Simple Lessons to Make Love Last* (Novato, CA: New World Library, 2004), 124-25.

9. Mark O'Connell, *The Marriage Benefit: The Surprising Rewards of Staying Together* (New York, NY: Springboard Press, 2008), 4.

10. Stanley, 9.

11. Gary Chapman, *The Marriage You've Always Wanted* (Chicago, IL: Moody Publishers, 2009), 55.

12. Robertson McQuilkin, *A Promise Kept* (Wheaton, IL: Tyndale House Publishers, 1998), 22.
13. Ibid., 30-31.
14. Ibid., 31.
15. Ibid., 51-52.
16. Ibid., 67.
17. Ibid., 18-19.

Chapter Six

1. "Top 30 Soulmate Quote with Pictures," *SayingImages*, June 9, 2015, accessed September 4, 2015, http://sayingimages.com/soulmate-quotes-pictures/.

Chapter Seven

2. *Goodreads*, accessed September 1, 2015, http://www.goodreads.com/quotes/search?utf8=%E2%93&q=Let+your+faith+be+bigger+than+your+fears&commit=search
3. Keller, 72.
4. Sky News US Team, "Philip Seymour Hoffman Died From Drugs Mix," *Sky News*, February 28, 2014, accessed September 4, 2015, http://news.sky.com/story/1219150/philip-seymour-hoffman-died-from-drugs-mix.
5. Jason Wachob, "John Lennon on Happiness," *Mindbodygreen.com*, May 23, 2011, accessed September 4, 2015, http://www.mindbodygreen.com/0-2471/John-Lennon-on-Happiness.html.
6. Phillips, Noelle, "Colorado Sheriffs Keep Popping Up in Spotlight," *The Gazette* (Colorado Springs, CO), July 6, 2014, B-1.

Notes

7. Mandi Woodruff and Michael B. Kelley, "20 Lottery Winners Who Blew It All." *Business Insider*, December 14, 2013, accessed September 4, 2015, http://www.businessinsider.com/lottery-winners-who-lost-everything-2013-12?op=1.

8. Ibid.

9. *Home Run*, directed by David Boyd (2013; Los Angeles, CA: Samuel Goldwyn Films and Provident Films, 2013), DVD.

Chapter Eight

1. Proverbs 31, "It's not the absence of conflict that determines the health of my relationships...," *Twitter*, accessed September 4, 2015, https://twitter.com/proverbs31org/status/486962594696400896.

2. "Radar," *Wikipedia*, accessed September 4, 2015, https://en.wikipedia.org/wiki/Radar.

3. Hendricks, 43.

4. Lauer, 184.

5. Greg Sabin, "10 People Who Made a Fortune During the Depression," *Mental_Floss*, August 12, 2009, accessed September 4, 2015, http://mentalfloss.com/article/22504/10-people-who-made-fortune-during-depression#.U8a90-3na1s.

6. Stanley, 122.

7. "Refurbished The Perfect Chair Zero Gravity Recliner by Human Touch." *Vitality Web*, accessed September 4, 2015, http://vitalityweb.com/backstore/perfect-chair.htm.

8. Keller, 115.

9. Lauer, 81.

10. O'Connell, 56.

11. Lauer, 72.

Chapter Nine

1. *Iz Quotes*, accessed September 4, 2015, http://izquotes.com/quote/288940.

2. Keller, 119-20.

3. Lauer, 87.

4. Keller, 108.

5. Ronn Elmore, *An Outrageous Commitment: The 48 Vows of an Indestructible Marriage*, (New York, NY: HarperCollins Publishers, 2003), 13.

6. Jerry Jenkins, *Hedges: Loving Your Marriage Enough to Protect It*, (Wheaton, IL: Crossway Books, 2005), 58.

7. Rosberg, 191.

8. Jenkins, 95.

9. Ibid., 95-96.

10. Ibid., 102.

11. Ibid., 103.

12. "Castle," *Wikipedia*, accessed September 4, 2015, http://en.wikipedia.org/wiki/Castle.

13. Gary Smalley, *I Promise: How Five Commitments Determine the Destiny of Your Marriage* (Nashville, TN: Thomas Nelson, 2006), 16.

14. Benjamin Davidson, *The Analytical Hebrew and Chaldee Lexicon of the Old Testament* (Mac Dill AFB, FL: MacDonald Publishing Co), 533.

15. O'Connell, 84-85.

16. Ibid., 85.. Ibid., 84-86.

17. Rosberg, 253.

18. Ibid., 254.

Notes

Chapter Ten

1. *Thequotepedia*.com, accessed September 4, 2015, http://www.thequotepedia.com/images/30/dont-ever-stop-dating-your-wife-and-dont-ever-stop-flirting-with-your-husband.png.
2. Alan Loy McGinnis, "How to Weather Marital Storms," *Reader's Digest,* April 1983, 53.
3. Smalley, 29.
4. Elmore, 119.
5. O'Connell, 197-98.
6. Stanley, 191.
7. Snalley, 183.
8. Chapman, 55.
9. Rosberg, 134-135.
10. Keller, 47.
11. Lauer, 123.
12. Bruce Larson, *No Longer Strangers* (Nashville, TN: Word Publishing Group, 1985), 116-117.

Chapter Eleven

1. Ryan Hodgson, "Change by Chapters," March 23, 2015, accessed September 4, 2015, http://www.ryanintheus.com/change-by-chapters/.
2. Garrison Wells, "Wildfire Experts Share Insight into Black Forest Fire and Importance of Mitigation," *The Gazette* (Colorado Springs, CO), February 9, 2014.
3. Ryan Maye Handy, "Colorado man's controlled burn triggers evacuations," *Wildfire Today*, March 29, 2015, accessed September 4, 2015, http://wildfiretoday.com/tag/colorado-springs/.

4. Stanley, 112.
5. Ibid., 119.
6. George W. Bush, *Decision Points* (New York, NY: Crown Publishers, 2010), 312.
7. Barbara McCarragher, "Hurricanes: History," *Mission 2010*, accessed September 4, 2015, http://web.mit.edu/12.000/www/m2010/finalwebsite/background/hurricanes/history.html.
8. Ibid.
9. Pam and Bill Farrel, "Family Fast Lane And Other Stages Of Married Life," *Thriving Family* (August/September 2014), 41.
10. Ibid., 42.
11. Daryl Chen, "The Brave Among Us," *Reader's Digest*, January 2014, 71.
12. Keller, 87.

Chapter Twelve

1. "Karen Salmansohn," *Tumblr*, January 8, 2015, accessed September 4, 2015, http://karensalmansohnauthor.tumblr.com/post/107528683187/in-the-end-we-wont-remember-the-most-beautiful.
2. Rosberg, 230-31.

Acknowledgments

While writing, in some respects, is a solitary experience, it truly never takes place in isolation. Bouncing ideas off of colleagues, gleaning valuable insights from the experiences of my clients and students, and relying on the support of key people is always a part of bringing a project, such as this, to completion. I would be remiss if I did not gratefully acknowledge at least a few of the many who have been a part of this endeavor.

Some of the best suggestions and advice that I have received as it relates to the publishing industry, continues to be my friend Paul Batura. An amazing author, as well as VP at *Focus on the Family*, Paul is one of the most humble and consistently giving individuals I know. I am grateful for his expertise and his support.

Having friends who are available for honest, creative, soul-searching discussion and objectivity is invaluable. While there are several, I especially want to acknowledge Brent Williams. Working in the field of hurting marriages, he understands the need for *Unstuck* and has offered insightful perspectives. Thank you for your feedback, your humor, and your friendship.

I want to express my appreciation to Ronda, John, Sierra, Jennifer and all of the team at Destiny Image who continue to believe in my writing and my passion to help strengthen marriages through this medium.

While staying "unstuck" requires diligence and perseverance, it is markedly easier when you have a partner fully engaged in the quest with you. I am blessed beyond measure to have a wife who is that partner. Andee graciously reads every word that I write, spotting my typos, but more importantly, willingly discussing ideas and concepts, and helping me to refine and clarify my thinking. She is marvelous at giving perspective through the eyes of the reader. But best of all – she is my confidant, soul-mate, and my friend. There is no person on the planet I would rather hang out with. Thanks for your love, support, and for never letting go as we journey together.

Finally, I am blessed, as a flawed and broken individual, to serve a God of second chances – who loves me, forgives me, and uses me —frailties and all. I am humbled and grateful by the overwhelming depth of His grace and love. None of this would happen apart from Him.

About the Author

BARRY HAM is an educator in a variety of forms: as a college professor, a Marriage and Family Therapist in practice in Colorado Springs, as well as an author and speaker.

He received his BA and BS degrees in ministry and music from Dallas Christian College. His first graduate degree was an MS in Psychology from Abilene Christian University, followed by a Masters in Marriage and Family Counseling from California State University. Finally, he received his Ph.D. in Clinical Psychology from Southern California University.

He was born in Tulsa, Oklahoma and was raised there and in Houston, Texas. He currently lives in the Colorado Springs area with his wife and two golden-doodles. He also has two grown children who also live in Colorado. Dr. Ham is available to speak at your church or gathering and is also available for Weekend Seminars

For booking and additional information, he can be contacted at:

Dr. Barry D. Ham
c/o Integrative Family/Individual Therapy
P.O. Box 63241
Colorado Springs, CO. 80962
drbdham@msn.com
www.ifithearppy.com

JOIN the CLUB

As a member of the **Love to Read Club**, receive exclusive offers for FREE, 99¢ and $1.99 e-books* every week. Plus, get the **latest news** about upcoming releases from **top authors** like these...

DESTINYIMAGE.COM/FREEBOOKS

T.D. JAKES | BILL JOHNSON | CINDY TRIMM | JIM STOVALL | BENI JOHNSON | MYLES MUNROE

*Prices valid in U.S. only. E-book offers available for a limited time each week. Amazon Kindle format only.